A Sourcebook for Christian Worship

a
sourcebook
for

CHRISTIAN WORSHIP

compiled
and
edited
by

PAUL S. McELROY

THE WORLD PUBLISHING COMPANY
CLEVELAND AND NEW YORK

Published by The World Publishing Company
2231 West 110th Street, Cleveland, Ohio 44102

Published simultaneously in Canada by Nelson, Foster & Scott, Ltd.

Library of Congress Catalog Card Number: 68–17647

Printed in the United States of America

ACKNOWLEDGMENTS

The Bible text in this publication is from the Revised Standard
Version of the Bible, *copyrighted 1946 and 1952 by the Division of
Christian Education of the National Council of Churches, and used
by permission.*

Acknowledgment is made to the following sources for the works in-
dicated.

ABINGDON PRESS, *for selections from*
   Acts of Worship, by W. B. J. Martin. Copyright © 1960 by Abing-
   don Press;
   Lift Up Your Hearts, by Walter Russell Bowie. Copyright ©
   1939, 1956 by Pierce and Washabaugh. Used by permission;
   Worship Programs, by Alice Anderson Bays. Copyright 1938,
   Abingdon Press.

THE ANGLICAN CHURCH OF CANADA, *for selections from*
   THE BOOK OF COMMON PRAYER OF THE ANGLICAN CHURCH OF
   CANADA, 1959.

APPLETON-CENTURY-CROFTS, *for selections from*
   Prayer for the Christian Year, by Charles Morris Addison. Copyright 1931 by Appleton-Century-Crofts.

ASSOCIATION PRESS, *for selections from*
   Resources for Worship, by Clarice M. Bowman. Copyright 1961,
   National Board of Young Men's Christian Associations.

THE BETHANY PRESS, *for selections from*
   Christian Worship: A Service Book, edited by G. Edwin Osborn.
   Copyright 1953, by William H. Cramblet, Christian Board of
   Publication.

iv

WILLIAM BLACKWOOD & SONS, LTD., Edinburgh, *for selections from* THE BOOK OF COMMON ORDER, 1896.

CAMBRIDGE UNIVERSITY PRESS, London, and The Publications Committee of the Episcopal Church of Scotland *for a selection from* THE SCOTTISH BOOK OF COMMON PRAYER, 1929.

CENTRAL CONFERENCE OF AMERICAN RABBIS, *for selections from* THE UNION PRAYER BOOK, newly revised edition, 1940.

THE CHICAGO THEOLOGICAL SEMINARY, *for selections from* A Manual of Meditation, 1926, prepared for use in The Thorndyke Hilton Memorial Chapel, The Chicago Theological Seminary.

THE CHURCH OF ENGLAND, Central Board of Finance, *for selections from* PRAYER BOOK AS PROPOSED IN 1928, printed with permission of the holders of the copyright.

CHURCH OF IRELAND, Standing Committee of the General Synod, *for selections from* THE BOOK OF COMMON PRAYER OF THE CHURCH OF IRELAND.

CHURCH OF SCOTLAND, Department of Publicity and Publication, *for selections from* A BOOK OF SERVICES AND PRAYERS.

CHURCH OF SOUTH INDIA, the Synod, *for selections from* THE BOOK OF COMMON WORSHIP OF THE CHURCH OF SOUTH INDIA, with permission also of Oxford University Press, Bombay, Publishers.

DEVIN-ADAIR COMPANY, *for selections from* Eastern Catholic Worship, by Donald Attwater, published and copyrighted 1945 by the Devin-Adair Company, reprinted by permission.

DOUBLEDAY & COMPANY, INC., *for selections from* The Dead Sea Scriptures, by Theodor H. Gaster. Copyright © 1956, 1964, by Theodor H. Gaster.

E. P. DUTTON & CO., INC., *for selections from* BOOK OF COMMON WORSHIP, edited by Bishop Wilbur P. Thirkield and Dr. Oliver Huckle. Copyright, 1932, by E. P. Dutton & Co., Inc. Renewal © 1960 by Gilbert H. Thirkield; The Temple, by W. E. Orchard, copyright, 1918, E. P. Dutton & Co., Inc. Renewal, 1946, by W. E. Orchard; A Chain of Prayer Across the Ages, compiled by Selina F. Fox. Published by E. P. Dutton & Co., Inc. Reprinted with their permission and also that of John Murray, Ltd., London; Devotional Services, by Rev. John Hunter, D.D. Published by E. P. Dutton & Co., Inc., and reprinted with their permission.

EDEN PUBLISHING HOUSE, *for selections from* Evangelical Book of Worship, 1916. Used by permission.

Acknowledgments

HARPER & ROW, *for selections by*
Arthur W. Cleaves, W. Earl Ledden, James Dalton Morrison, and others, in *Minister's Service Book*, 1937, edited by James Dalton Morrison and Charles L. Wallis;
The Book of English Collects, 1940, edited by John Wallace Suter, Jr.;
Communion With God, 1922, by Elmore McNeill McKee;
Thanks Be To God, 1960, by Robert N. Rodenmeyer;
Let Us Worship God, by Hubert L. Simpson, used by permission;
The Imitation of Christ, by Thomas à Kempis (Whitford-Klein Edition), 1943.

INDEPENDENT PRESS, LTD., London, *for selections from*
A Book of Services and Prayers, published 1959 for the Congregational Union of England and Wales.

INTERNATIONAL JOURNAL OF RELIGIOUS EDUCATION, *for*
a poem by Betty Jane and J. Martin Bailey. Copyright 1964, Division of Christian Education, National Council of Churches; a passage by Oscar J. Rumpf, copyright 1964, Division of Christian Education, National Council of Churches. Used by permission of publisher and author.

THE JUDSON PRESS, Valley Forge, Pa., *for selections from*
The Life I Owe, by William J. Keech, 1963.

ALFRED A. KNOPF, INC., *for selections from*
The Prophet, by Kahlil Gibran, with permission of the publishers, Alfred A. Knopf, Inc. Copyright 1923 by Kahlil Gibran; renewal copyright 1951 by administrators C. T. A. of Kahlil Gibran estate and Mary G. Gibran.

LONGMANS, GREEN & CO., LTD., London, *for selections from*
An Anthology of Prayers, by A. S. T. Fisher, 1934. Also by permission of A. S. T. Fisher;
Home Prayers 1900, by James Martineau.

LUTHERAN CHURCH IN AMERICA, *for selections from*
Service Book and Hymnal, copyright 1958, used by permission of Commission on Liturgy and Hymnal.

THE MACMILLAN COMPANY, *for selections from*
A Church Service Book, a prayer by S. Arthur Devin;
The Cost of Discipleship, 1948, by Dietrich Bonhoeffer;
The Widow of Bye Street, 1912, by John Masefield;
Prayers for Private and Family Use, by Charles Lewis Slattery, 1922.

THE METHODIST PUBLISHING HOUSE, *for selections from*
The Book of Worship, 1952, a prayer by Lisgar R. Eckhardt.

METHUEN & CO., LTD., London, Publishers, *for selections from*
Preces Privatae, 1930, by Lancelot Andrewes.

JEANNE HATCH MICKIE, *for selections from*
"Open Door," a poem, in *Newsletter of the Disciplined Order of Christ*, Vol. II, Oct. 1953.

MOREHOUSE-BARLOW CO., INC., *for selections from*
The Book of Collects, by Francis Lightbourne, used by permission of Morehouse-Barlow Co.;
Book of Offices and Prayers, 1929, and from BOOK OF COMMON PRAYER, 1929.

IVAN OBOLENSKY, INC., *for*
The Prayers of Man, compiled by Alphonso M. di Nola. Copyright © 1961 by Ivan Obolensky, Inc. Reprinted by permission.

OXFORD UNIVERSITY PRESS, New York, London and Bombay, *for selections from*
The Kingdom, the Power and the Glory. Copyright 1933, by Oxford University Press, Inc., and renewed 1961 by Bradford Young;
BOOK OF COMMON ORDER (1928 edition), by permission of the Committee on Public Worship and Aids to Devotion of the Church of Scotland, and Oxford University Press;
A Source Book of Christian Worship, by Huxtable, Marsh, Micklem and Todd. Copyright. Reprinted from *A Book of Public Worship* by permission of Oxford University Press;
An Outline of Christian Worship, 1936, by William D. Maxwell;
THE BOOK OF PUBLIC WORSHIP, 1946, with permission of Covener of the Publications Committee, the Presbyterian Church of England;
THE BOOK OF COMMON WORSHIP OF THE CHURCH OF SOUTH INDIA, Oxford University Press, Bombay, Publishers.

THE PILGRIM PRESS, *for selections from*
The Pilgrim Hymnal. Copyright 1931, 1935, The Pilgrim Press. Used by permission;
Book of Church Services, 1922;
Pulpit and Parish Manual, prepared by Henry Hallam Saunderson, 1930;
The Fellowship of Prayer, Lenten Season, 1932, by Dwight J. Bradley;
The Fellowship of Prayer, Feb. 13, 1964 prayer by James E. Wagner;
The Fellowship of Prayer, Lenten Season, 1965. Copyright 1964, The Pilgrim Press;
Church Worship Book, by Charles Wolcott Merriam;
A Book of Worship for Free Churches, prayers by Boynton Merrill. Oxford University Press, New York. Copyright 1948 by the Board of Home Missions of the Congregational Churches. Used by permission.

THE PRESBYTERIAN CHURCH, *for*
THE BOOK OF COMMON WORSHIP, the Board of Christian Education of the Presbyterian Church, U.S.A., Philadelphia, Pa.

THE PRESBYTERIAN CHURCH OF ENGLAND, *for selections from*
DIRECTORY FOR PUBLIC WORSHIP, 1946, with permission of Covener of Publications.

PUTNAM'S-COWARD-McCANN, *for selections from*
Moses. Copyright 1951 by Sholem Asch, used with permission, G. P. Putnam's Sons;

Acknowledgments

> *In the Steps of St. Francis*, 1939, by Ernest Raymond, published by H. C. Kinsey and Company, Inc. Used with permission.

FLEMING H. REVELL COMPANY, *for selections from*
> *The Minister's Book of Prayers*, by Charles Carroll Albertson, 1941;
> *The Minister's Service Handbook*, by James L. Christensen, 1960.

THE SEABURY PRESS, *for selections from*
> *Key Words for Lent*, by George W. Barrett, 1963, The Seabury Press.

CHARLES SCRIBNER'S SONS, *for*
> *The Poems of Henry Van Dyke*, by Henry Van Dyke. Charles Scribner's Sons, 1902;
> *A Diary of Private Prayer*, by John Baillie, 1955, with permission of Charles Scribner's Sons, publishers.

STUDENT CHRISTIAN MOVEMENT PRESS, LTD., London, *for selections from*
> *The Book of Prayers for Schools*, by Hugh Martin, ed., 1936, The Student Christian Movement Press, Ltd. (SCM).

THE UNITED CHURCH OF CANADA, *for selections from*
> THE BOOK OF COMMON ORDER.

THE VIKING PRESS, INC., *for selections from*
> *The Dead Sea Scrolls*, by Millar Burrows. Copyright © 1955, by Millar Burrows. Used with permission.

THE WESTMINSTER PRESS, *for selections from*
> 1890 edition of *Euchologian*, A BOOK OF COMMON ORDER, used in 1946 edition of BOOK OF COMMON WORSHIP.

Contents

Preface

This anthology provides resources for each stage in the service of worship. Although other collections of prayers and aids are currently available, the leader planning a full service must search for materials scattered through a number of reference works. By arranging selections from the Bible and traditional and contemporary sources in a pattern that follows the usual sequence of worship, from Prayers Before Services to Benedictions, the editor has sought to fill a need felt by most ministers and others who do not have access to large libraries. The value that may be found in this collection, then, will lie in its combination of convenient and compact form with comprehensive selection of passages suitable to special parts of worship.

Such "A Sourcebook for Christian Worship," intended for use by various free communions or denominations, naturally includes a larger variety of services than any single denominational book. What is here presented are significant expressions of prayer and worship that can be used by members of Christian churches throughout the world.

The Biblical quotations are taken primarily from the Authorized Version or the Revised Standard Version; where other translations are used, this has been noted. The sources of other items include works from most major traditions within the Christian heritage, from the first century into the twentieth. It is hoped that the range and variety of the material may serve an ecumenical purpose, enabling worshippers to receive enrichment from the vast legacy of Christian prayer and praise.

An extensive topical index (p. 235) is provided to enable the user to select passages especially suitable for special themes and occasions.

A diligent effort has been made to trace selections to their primary sources and to give proper credit in the Acknowledgments (p. iv). This has proved to be a considerable task, however, and the editor would welcome additional information from readers who may recognize the source for a given selection. An abbreviated source line has been given for convenience at the end of each passage, but the reader should consult the more detailed acknowledgments for full information.

Editors seem to follow no uniform procedures in the matter of punctuation. Some use semi-colons, others use periods; some prefer capitals to small case when "Thy" is an adjective referring to God; some adhere to the ancient spelling of such words as "honour" and "Saviour"; others omit the "u." In the interest of accuracy in quotation I have tried in most cases to respect the forms used in the sources from which they are taken.

I am deeply grateful to the many authors, publishers, and copyright owners whose courtesy and generous cooperation has made this book possible. I extend a very special thanks to my secretary, Mrs. Else Gissenaas; to the members of the First Congregational Church of St. Louis; to my wife Clara B. McElroy, and my daughter Barbara; and to the staff of the religious books department of The World Publishing Company for encouragement and invaluable assistance.

This book is offered in the sincere hope that it will provide a welcome sourcebook for worship leaders and that it will prove a means of enriching services of corporate worship.

Paul Simpson McElroy

A Sourcebook for Christian Worship

I

Prayers
Before Services

1   O God of Beauty, we would lift our hearts as well as our voices in praise to Thee, praying that the words of our mouths and the meditations of our hearts may always be acceptable in Thy sight, O Lord, our Strength and our Redeemer.

2   Grant us, O Lord, the help of thy Spirit in our hearts, that we may enter into thy holy presence with reverence and gladness and render a service acceptable unto thee.

3   Eternal and ever-blessed God, who art worthy to receive greater praise than we can either give or understand; be pleased to bless this congregation with Thy Holy Spirit, that it may impart to us thoughts higher than our own thoughts, prayers better than our own prayers, and powers beyond our own powers; and grant to Thy servant our minister that, by the same Holy Spirit, he may be given both liberty and constraint in the Gospel, that we may know that Thou art in the midst of us, hear Thy Word, and worship Thee in spirit and in truth.

H. F. Leatherland

4   We thank Thee, O God, for the gift of song and for the joy it brings to all Thy children everywhere. Accept the hymns and anthems which we offer to Thee in our worship as expressions of hearts that are filled to overflowing with joy for Thy great goodness toward us, through Jesus Christ our Lord.

5   Our heavenly Father; here, on the threshold of this service, we remember all who like ourselves are about to enter into thy holy presence; all our brethren in Christ for whom this day is the Lord's Day, and this hour the hour of worship. Help them, and help us, to be glad in thee. Grant them, and grant us, the abundance of thy mercy. And to thy ministers in every place, as to thy servant here, give wisdom and grace, that they may worthily preach the Gospel of our Lord Jesus, comfort thy people with thy Word, and quicken the hearts and minds of men and women in devotion to thee, to the glory of thy holy name.

A Book of Services and Prayers

6   O God, we pray that this service of praise and prayer may be enriched through song. May we upon whom leadership in this service falls, enter humbly, reverently, and joyfully. Give us pure hearts with lives as well as voices dedicated to thy service.

7   O Lord, open thou our lips and purify our hearts; that we may worthily magnify thy holy name.

Dean Milner White

8   O Thou Great Creator, who madest man that he should praise Thee with his whole being, we come before Thee to sing Thy praises with our whole hearts. May this service be for us, O Lord, a giving of our whole selves through song in praise to Thee. Praise ye the Lord, for it is good to sing praises unto the Lord our God.

9   Our Father, as we gather together to sing Thy praises, we would pray that we may so live that our lives as well as our voices may be in tune with one another and with Thee.

10   O Thou, who hast given to us such gifts of speech and of song as we have; we would offer them together with the love of our hearts, unto Thee. Use them, and us, we pray Thee, to the glory of Thy Name.

Boynton Merrill

11   Holy Father, who callest us to serve Thee in the worship of Thy house; grant us so to praise Thee with our hearts as with our voices, that the souls of the assembled with us may be uplifted, purified, and strengthened; and that they and we together may be confirmed in faith and love to Thee, through Jesus Christ our Lord. Amen.

Book of Common Order, Scotland

12   O God, to whom we would lift our hearts as well as our lips in praise, grant that we may practice in our lives what we proclaim in our songs. For the privilege of leading others in the conduct of worship we are grateful and we would ask that all we do may be in harmony with thy will.

Paul S. McElroy

13   O Heavenly Father, as we go into thy house cleanse our hearts and help us to worship thee in spirit and in truth. Keep our minds from idle and worldly thoughts, and grant that the prayers and praises of thy people may go up from thy holy temple on earth to thy mercy seat in heaven.

Book of Common Worship

14   O God, who hast given us minds to know thee, hearts to love thee, voices to show forth thy praise; help us to worship thee with understanding, reverence, and joy, and grant that in this service we may both receive thy blessing and be made a blessing to others; for the sake of Jesus Christ our Lord.

A Book of Services and Prayers

15   Grant, O God, that as we lead the praises of others, we may ourselves gladly and thankfully worship thee; and help us as we lead the prayers of others, to come before thee with reverent and prayerful spirit; so that the words of our mouths and the meditations of our hearts may be acceptable in thy sight.

A Book of Services and Prayers

16   Cleanse our hearts, we humbly beseech thee, O Lord, from all vain and wandering thoughts; that we may joyfully praise thee in thy holy house, through Jesus Christ our Lord.

Dean Milner White

17   So often, O Lord, we sing to thee with hollow hearts, although we have so much to be thankful for. Our indifference too often blocks out what sincere worshipful expressions might arise. Help us to be sensitive to thy presence in this hour of worship not only for our own needs but that we may contribute to an atmosphere in which others may also find thee. We thank thee for this opportunity to praise thee.

Barbara B. McElroy

18   O God who hast given us minds to know Thee, hearts to love Thee, and voices to show forth thy praise; give us grace, we beseech Thee, to dedicate ourselves freely to thy service, that we may reverently fulfill the worship of thy

4

sanctuary, and beautify the praises of thy house, through Jesus Christ our Lord. Amen.

Book of Common Order, Scotland

19   Open Thou our lips, O Lord, and our mouths show forth Thy praise. Inspire those here who have consecrated to Thy service the gift of song. And so sustain them in their guidance of the congregation who are now met to praise Thee, that Thy name may be glorified, and Thy people truly rejoice in Thy presence with psalms. Help them so to bear themselves as they worship Thee in Thy sanctuary that they shall be acceptable to Thee in this our office, and make all Thy people joyful.

Let Us Worship God

20   Grant, O Lord, that we may so enter thy courts and so wait before thee now that our worship may be acceptable unto thee.

Boynton Merrill

21   O God, our heavenly Father, who hast called us to the sacred ministry of praise in the service of Thy church, make us ready now to worship Thee in spirit and in truth. Teach us to understand and love Thy holy service and help us to be reverent and attentive, guarding us from all wandering thoughts and unseemly actions, and make all that we shall say and do acceptable unto Thee.

Book of Common Worship

II

Calls
To Worship
and
Opening
Sentences

This section of Calls to Worship and Opening Sentences includes selections that might also be described as Invitations to Worship and Ascriptions of Praise. A *Call to Worship,* according to Henry Sloane Coffin, is an invitation to the congregation to worship God. It is therefore never addressed to God, but rather to the people. Words spoken directly to God belong, not in the Call, but in a prayer. *Opening Sentences* or *Invitations to Worship* serve a similar purpose, expressing adoration and praise. Usually, these are statements reminding people of the holiness and greatness of God, and their usage implies that the people have come together for the express purpose of worshiping God.

Ascriptions of Praise (p. 48) are more commonly directed to God, but said before the people as a means of praise to God and suitable for use at the beginning of worship.

A. FROM THE OLD TESTAMENT

1   Surely the Lord is in this place; . . . This is none other than the house of God, and this is the gate of heaven.
Genesis 28:16–17

2   I am the Lord your God, who brought you out of the house of bondage. You shall have no other gods before me. You shall not make yourself a graven image, or any likeness of anything that is in heaven above, or that is in the earth beneath, or that is in the water under the earth; you shall not bow down to them or serve them; for I the Lord your God am a jealous God, visiting the iniquity of the fathers upon the children to the third and the fourth generation of those who hate me, but showing steadfast love to thousands of those who love me and keep my commandments.
Exodus 20:2–6

3   Remember the sabbath day, to keep it holy.
Exodus 20:8

4   You shall not hate your brother in your heart, but you shall reason with your neighbor, lest you bear sin because of him. You shall not take vengeance or bear any grudge against the sons of your own people, but you shall love your neighbor as yourself; I am the Lord. You shall keep my statutes.
Leviticus 19:17–19

5   You will seek the Lord your God, and you will find him, if you search after him with all your heart and with all your soul . . . for the Lord your God is a merciful God; he will not fail you or destroy you or forget the covenant with your fathers which he swore to them.
Deuteronomy 4:29–31

6   Hear, O Israel: The Lord our God is one Lord, and you shall love the Lord your God with all your heart, and with all your soul, and with all your might. And these words

which I command you this day shall be upon your heart; and you shall teach them diligently to your children, and shall talk of them when you sit in your house, and when you walk by the way, and when you lie down, and when you rise. And you shall bind them as a sign upon your hand, and they shall be as frontlets between your eyes. And you shall write them on the doorposts of your house and on your gates.

Deuteronomy 6:4–9

7　All the commandment which I command you this day you shall be careful to do, that you may live and multiply. . . . And you shall remember all the way which the Lord your God has led you . . . that he might humble you, testing you to know what was in your heart, whether you would keep his commandments, or not.

Deuteronomy 8:1–2

8　You shall rejoice in all the good which the Lord your God has given to you and to your house, you . . . and the sojourner who is among you.

Deuteronomy 26:11

9　Ascribe greatness to our God! The Rock, his work is perfect; for all his ways are justice. A God of faithfulness and without iniquity, just and right is he.

Deuteronomy 32:3–4

10　There is none like God . . . who rides through the heavens to your help, and in his majesty through the skies. The eternal God is your dwelling place, and underneath are the everlasting arms.

Deuteronomy 33:26–27

11　Have I not commanded you? Be strong and of good courage; be not frightened, neither be dismayed; for the Lord your God is with you wherever you go.

Joshua 1:9

12　Now therefore fear the Lord, and serve him in sincerity and in faithfulness.

Joshua 24:14

13   Choose this day whom you will serve . . . but as for me and my house, we will serve the Lord.

The Lord our God we will serve, and his voice we will obey.

Joshua 24:15–24

14   The Lord our God be with us, as he was with our fathers; may he not leave us or forsake us; that he may incline our hearts to him, to walk in all his ways, and to keep his commandments, his statutes, and his ordinances, which he commanded our fathers.

I Kings 8:57–58

15   O give thanks to the Lord, call on his name, make known his deeds among the peoples! Sing to him, sing praises to him, tell of all his wonderful works! Glory in his holy name; let the hearts of those who seek the Lord rejoice!

I Chronicles 16:8–10

16   Seek the Lord and his strength, seek his presence continually! Remember the wonderful works that he has done, the wonders he wrought, the judgments he uttered.

I Chronicles 16:11–12

17   Sing to the Lord, all the earth! Tell of his salvation from day to day. Declare his glory among the nations, his marvelous works among all the peoples! For great is the Lord, and greatly to be praised.

I Chronicles 16:23–25

18   O give thanks to the Lord, for he is good; for his steadfast love endures for ever!

I Chronicles 16:34

19   Thine, O Lord, is the greatness, and the power, and the glory, and the victory, and the majesty; for all that is in the heavens and in the earth is thine; thine is the kingdom, O Lord, and thou art exalted as head above all. Both riches and honor come from thee and thou rulest over all. In thy hand are power and might; and in thy hand it is to make

great and to give strength to all. And now we thank thee, our God, and praise thy glorious name.

I Chronicles 29:11–13

20   If my people who are called by my name humble themselves, and pray and seek my face, and turn from their wicked ways, then I will hear from heaven, and will forgive their sin and heal their land. Now my eyes will be open and my ears attentive to the prayer that is made in this place.

II Chronicles 7:14–15

21   The Lord your God is gracious and merciful and will not turn away his face from you, if you return to him.

II Chronicles 30:9

22   Agree with God, and be at peace; thereby good will come to you.

Job 22:21

23   I will give thanks to the Lord with my whole heart;
I will tell of all thy wonderful deeds.
I will be glad and exult in thee,
I will sing praise to thy name, O Most High.

Psalms 9:1–2

24   The Lord is a stronghold for the oppressed,
A stronghold in times of trouble.
And those who know thy name put their trust in thee,
For thou, O Lord, hast not forsaken those who seek
thee.

Psalms 9:9–10

25   O Lord, who shall sojourn in thy tent?
Who shall dwell on thy holy hill?
He who walks blamelessly, and does what is right,
And speaks truth from his heart.

Psalms 15:1–2

26   The Lord is my rock, and my fortress, and my deliverer,
My God, my rock, in whom I take refuge,
My shield, and the horn of my salvation, my stronghold.

Psalms 18:2

27 For who is God, but the Lord?
And who is a rock, except our God?
The God who girded me with strength;
And made my feet like hinds' feet,
And set me secure on the heights.

Psalms 18:31–33

28 The heavens are telling the glory of God;
and the firmament proclaims his handiwork.
Day to day pours forth speech,
and night to night declares knowledge.
There is no speech, nor are there words;
their voice is not heard;
Yet their voice goes out through all the earth,
and their words to the end of the world.

Psalms 19:1–4

29 The law of the Lord is perfect, reviving the soul;
The testimony of the Lord is sure, making wise the
simple;
The precepts of the Lord are right, rejoicing the heart;
The commandment of the Lord is pure, enlightening
the eyes;
The fear of the Lord is clean, enduring for ever;
The ordinances of the Lord are true, and righteous
altogether,
More to be desired are they than gold, even much fine
gold;
Sweeter also than honey and drippings of the
honeycomb.

Psalms 19:7–10

30 All the ends of the earth shall remember and turn to
the Lord;
And all the families of the nations shall worship
before Him.
For dominion belongs to the Lord, and he rules over
the nations.

Psalms 22:27–28

31 The earth is the Lord's and the fulness thereof,
The world and those who dwell therein;

For he has founded it upon the seas,
    and established it upon the rivers.

Psalms 24:1–2

32 Who shall ascend the hill of the Lord?
        And who shall stand in his holy place?
    He who has clean hands and a pure heart,
        who does not lift up his soul to what is false,
        and does not swear deceitfully.
    He will receive blessing from the Lord,
        and vindication from the God of his salvation.

Psalms 24:3–5

33 The Lord is my light and my salvation;
        whom shall I fear?
    The Lord is the stronghold of my life;
        of whom shall I be afraid.

Psalms 27:1

34 One thing have I asked of the Lord, that will I seek
        after;
    that I may dwell in the house of the Lord all the
        days of my life,
    to behold the beauty of the Lord, and to inquire in
        his temple.

Psalms: 27:4

35 Wait for the Lord:
        be strong, and let your heart take courage:
    Yea, wait for the Lord!

Psalms 27:14

36 Love the Lord, all you his saints!
    The Lord preserves the faithful, but abundantly
        requites him who acts haughtily.
    Be strong, and let your heart take courage, all you
        who wait for the Lord.

Psalms 31:23–24

37 For the word of the Lord is upright;
        and all his work is done in faithfulness.
    He loves righteousness and justice;
        the earth is full of the steadfast love of the Lord.

Psalms 33:4–5

38   Blessed is the nation whose God is the Lord,
       the people whom he has chosen as his heritage!

Psalms 33:12

39   Our soul waits for the Lord;
       he is our help and shield.
    Yea, our heart is glad in him,
       because we trust in his holy name.
    Let thy steadfast love, O Lord, be upon us,
       even as we hope in thee.

Psalms 33:20–22

40   I will bless the Lord at all times;
       his praise shall continually be in my mouth.
    My soul makes its boast in the Lord;
       let the afflicted hear and be glad.
    O magnify the Lord with me,
       and let us exalt his name together!

Psalms 34:1–3

41   Commit your way to the Lord;
       trust in him, and he will act.
    He will bring forth your vindication as the light,
       and your right as the noonday.
    Be still before the Lord, and wait patiently for him;
       fret not yourself over him who prospers in his way,
       over the man who carries out evil devices!

Psalms 37:5–7

42   Blessed is the man who makes the Lord his trust,
       who does not turn to the proud,
       to those who go astray after false gods!
    Thou hast multiplied, O Lord my God,
       thy wondrous deeds and thy thoughts toward us;
       none can compare with thee!
    Were I to proclaim and tell of them,
       they would be more than can be numbered.

Psalms 40:4–5

43   God is our refuge and strength,
       a very present help in trouble.
    Therefore we will not fear though the earth should
         change,
       though the mountains shake in the heart of the sea;

though its waters roar and foam,
though the mountains tremble with its tumult.

Psalms 46:1–3

44 Be still, and know that I am God.
I am exalted among the nations,
I am exalted in the earth!
The Lord of hosts is with us;
the God of Jacob is our refuge.

Psalms 46:10–11

45 We have thought on thy steadfast love, O God,
in the midst of thy temple.
As thy name, O God,
so thy praise reaches to the ends of the earth.
Thy right hand is filled with victory.

Psalms 48:9–10

46 The Mighty One, God the Lord,
speaks and summons the earth
from the rising of the sun to its setting.
Out of Zion, the perfection of beauty, God shines forth.

Psalms 50:1–2

47 Make a joyful noise to God, all the earth;
sing the glory of his name;
give to him glorious praise!

Psalms 66:1–2

48 Bless our God, O peoples,
let the sound of his praise be heard,
who has kept us among the living,
and has not let our feet slip.

Psalms 66:8–9

49 Let the peoples praise thee, O God;
let all the peoples praise thee!
Let the nations be glad and sing for joy,
for thou dost judge the peoples with equity
and guide the nations upon earth.
Let the peoples praise thee, O God;
let all the peoples praise thee!

Psalms 67:3–5

50 Let the peoples praise thee, O God;
    let all the peoples praise thee!
The earth has yielded its increase;
    God, our God, has blessed us.
God has blessed us;
    let all the ends of the earth fear him!

Psalms 67:5–7

51 Blessed be the Lord, the God of Israel,
    who alone does wondrous things.
Blessed be his glorious name for ever;
    may his glory fill the whole earth!
      Amen and Amen!

Psalms 72:18–19

52 How lovely is thy dwelling place,
    O Lord of hosts!
My soul longs, yea, faints
    for the courts of the Lord;
My heart and flesh sing for joy
    to the living God.

Psalms 84:1–2

53 Let me hear what God the Lord will speak,
    for he will speak peace to his people,
    to his saints,
    to those who turn to him in their hearts.
Surely his salvation is at hand for those who fear him,
    that glory may dwell in our land.

Psalms 85:8–9

54 He who dwells in the shelter of the Most High,
    who abides in the shadow of the Almighty,
    will say to the Lord, "My refuge and my fortress;
    my God, in whom I trust."

Psalms 91:1–2

55 It is good to give thanks to the Lord,
    to sing praises to thy name, O Most High;
to declare thy steadfast love in the morning,
    and thy faithfulness by night,

For thou, O Lord, hast made me glad by thy work;
   at the works of thy hands I sing for joy.

Psalms 92:1–2, 4

56   O come, let us sing to the Lord;
       let us make a joyful noise to the rock of our
           salvation!
   Let us come into his presence with thanksgiving;
       let us make a joyful noise to him with songs of
           praise!
   For the Lord is a great God,
       and a great King above all gods.

Psalms 95:1–3

57   O come, let us worship and bow down,
       let us kneel before the Lord, our Maker!
   For he is our God,
       and we are the people of his pasture,
       and the sheep of his hand.

Psalms 95:6–7

58   O sing to the Lord a new song;
       sing to the Lord, all the earth!
   Sing to the Lord, bless his name;
       tell of his salvation from day to day.
   Declare his glory among the nations,
       his marvelous works among all the peoples!
   For great is the Lord, and greatly to be praised.

Psalms 96:1–4

59   Make a joyful noise to the Lord, all the lands!
   Serve the Lord with gladness!
   Come into his presence with singing!
   Know that the Lord is God!
       It is he that made us, and we are his;
       we are his people, and the sheep of his pasture.
   Enter his gates with thanksgiving,
       and his courts with praise!
       Give thanks to him, bless his name!
   For the Lord is good;
       his steadfast love endures for ever,
       and his faithfulness to all generations.

Psalms 100:1–5

60 Bless the Lord, O my soul;
    and all that is within me, bless his holy name!
Bless the Lord, O my soul,
    and forget not all his benefits,
who forgives all your iniquity,
    who heals all your diseases,
who redeems your life from the Pit,
    who crowns you with steadfast love and mercy,
who satisfies you with good as long as you live
    so that your youth is renewed like the eagle's.
Psalms 103:1–5

61 But the steadfast love of the Lord is from everlasting
    to everlasting
    upon those who fear him,
    and his righteousness to children's children,
To those who keep his covenant
    and remember to do his commandments.
Psalms 103:17–18

62 Bless the Lord, all his hosts,
    his ministers that do his will!
Bless the Lord, all his works,
    in all places of his dominion.
Bless the Lord, O my soul!
Psalms 103:21–22

63 I will sing to the Lord as long as I live;
    I will sing praise to my God while I have being.
May my meditation be pleasing to him,
    for I rejoice in the Lord.
Psalms 104:33–34

64 O give thanks to the Lord, call on his name,
    make known his deeds among the peoples!
Sing to him, sing praises to him,
    tell of all his wonderful works!
Glory in his holy name;
    let the hearts of those who seek the Lord rejoice!
Seek the Lord and his strength,
    seek his presence continually!
Psalms 105:1–4

65   Praise the Lord!
 O give thanks to the Lord, for he is good;
  for his steadfast love endures for ever!

Psalms 106:1

66   Praise the Lord!
 I will give thanks to the Lord with my whole heart,
  in the company of the upright, in the congregation.
 Great are the works of the Lord,
  studied by all who have pleasure in them.
 Full of honor and majesty is his work,
  and his righteousness endures for ever.
 He has caused his wonderful works to be remembered;
  the Lord is gracious and merciful.

Psalms 111:1–4

67   Praise the Lord!
 Praise, O servants of the Lord,
  praise the name of the Lord!
 Blessed be the name of the Lord
  from this time forth and for evermore!
 From the rising of the sun to its setting
  the name of the Lord is to be praised!
 The Lord is high above all nations,
  and his glory above the heavens!

Psalms 113:1–4

68   What shall I render to the Lord
  for all his bounty to me?
 I will lift up the cup of salvation
  and call on the name of the Lord,
 I will pay my vows to the Lord
  in the presence of all his people.

Psalms 116:12–14

69   Praise the Lord, all nations!
 Extol him, all peoples!
 For great is his steadfast love toward us;
  and the faithfulness of the Lord endures for ever.
 Praise the Lord!

Psalms 117:1–2

70   This is the day which the Lord has made;
    let us rejoice and be glad in it.

Psalms 118:24

71   I lift up my eyes to the hills.
    From whence does my help come?
    My help comes from the Lord,
        who made heaven and earth.

Psalms 121:1–2

72   I was glad when they said to me,
    "Let us go to the house of the Lord!"

Psalms 122:1

73   Behold, how good and pleasant it is
        when brothers dwell in unity!
    It is like the precious oil upon the head,
        running down upon the beard,
    upon the beard of Aaron,
        running down on the collar of his robes!
    It is like the dew of Hermon
        which falls on the mountains of Zion!
    For there the Lord has commanded the blessing,
        life for evermore.

Psalms 133:1–3

74   Come, bless the Lord,
        all you servants of the Lord,
        who stand by night in the house of the Lord,
    Lift up your hands to the holy place,
        and bless the Lord!
    May the Lord bless you from Zion,
        he who made heaven and earth!

Psalms 134:1–3

75   Praise the Lord.
    Praise the name of the Lord,
        give praise, O servants of the Lord,
    you that stand in the house of the Lord,
        in the courts of the house of our God!
    Praise the Lord, for the Lord is good;
        sing to his name, for he is gracious!

Psalms 135:1–3

76 O give thanks to the Lord, for he is good,
  for his steadfast love endures for ever.
O give thanks to the God of gods,
  for his steadfast love endures for ever.
O give thanks to the Lord of lords,
  for his steadfast love endures for ever.

Psalms 136:1–3

77 Great is the Lord, and greatly to be praised,
  and his greatness is unsearchable.

Psalms 145:3

78 One generation shall laud thy works to another,
  and shall declare thy mighty acts.
Of the glorious splendor of thy majesty,
  and of thy wondrous works, I will meditate.

Psalms 145:4–5

79 The Lord is gracious and merciful,
  slow to anger and abounding in steadfast love.
The Lord is good to all,
  and his compassion is over all that he has made.

Psalms 145:8–9

80 All thy works shall give thanks to thee, O Lord,
  and all thy saints shall bless thee!
They shall speak of the glory of thy kingdom,
  and tell of thy power,
to make known to the sons of men thy mighty deeds,
  and the glorious splendor of thy kingdom.
Thy kingdom is an everlasting kingdom,
  and thy dominion endures throughout all generations.

Psalms 145:10–13

81 The Lord is just in all his ways,
  and kind in all his doings.
The Lord is near to all who call upon him,
  to all who call upon him in truth.

Psalms 145:17–18

82 Praise the Lord!
For it is good to sing praises to our God;
  for he is gracious, and a song of praise is seemly.
Psalms 147:1

83 Praise the Lord!
Praise the Lord from the heavens,
  praise him in the heights!
Praise him, all his angels
  praise him, all his host!
Psalms 148:1–2

84 Kings of the earth and all peoples,
  princes and all rulers of the earth!
Young men and maidens together,
  old men and children!
Let them praise the name of the Lord,
  for his name alone is exalted;
  his glory is above earth and heaven.
Psalms 148:11–13

85 Praise the Lord!
Sing to the Lord a new song,
  his praise in the assembly of the faithful!
Psalms 149:1

86 Praise the Lord!
Praise God in his sanctuary;
  praise him in his mighty firmament!
Praise him for his mighty deeds;
  praise him according to his exceeding greatness!
Let everything that breathes praise the Lord!
Praise the Lord!
Psalms 150:1–2, 6

87 Righteousness exalts a nation, but sin is a reproach
  to any people.
Proverbs 14:34

88 Come now, let us reason together, says the Lord:
  though your sins are like scarlet,
  they shall be as white as snow;

though they are red like crimson,
they shall become like wool.

Isaiah 1:18

89   Holy, holy, holy is the Lord of hosts;
the whole earth is full of his glory.

Isaiah 6:3

90   For to us a child is born, to us a son is given;
and the government will be upon his shoulder,
and his name will be called
Wonderful Counselor, Mighty God,
Everlasting Father, Prince of Peace.

Isaiah 9:6

91   Behold, God is my salvation;
I will trust, and will not be afraid;
for the Lord God is my strength and my song,
and he has become my salvation.

Isaiah 12:2

92   Give thanks to the Lord, call upon his name;
make known his deeds among the nations,
proclaim that his name is exalted.
Sing praises to the Lord, for he has done gloriously;
let this be known in all the earth.
Shout, and sing for joy, O inhabitant of Zion,
for great in your midst is the Holy One of Israel.

Isaiah 12:4–6

93   Thou dost keep him in perfect peace,
whose mind is stayed on thee,
because he trusts in thee.
Trust in the Lord for ever,
for the Lord God is an everlasting rock.

Isaiah 26:3–4

94   For thus said the Lord God, the Holy One of Israel
in returning and rest you shall be saved;
in quietness and in trust shall be your strength.

Isaiah 30:15

95   A voice cries:
In the wilderness prepare the way of the Lord,
    make straight in the desert a highway for our God.
Every valley shall be lifted up,
    and every mountain and hill be made low;
the uneven ground shall become level,
    and the rough places a plain.
And the glory of the Lord shall be revealed.

Isaiah 40:3–5

96   Have you not known? Have you not heard?
Has it not been told you from the beginning?
Have you not understood from the foundations of the
      earth?
It is he who sits above the circle of the earth,
    and its inhabitants are like grasshoppers;
who stretches out the heavens like a curtain,
    and spreads them like a tent to dwell in;
who brings princes to nought,
    and makes the rulers of the earth as nothing.

Isaiah 40:21–23

97   Have you not known? Have you not heard?
The Lord is the everlasting God,
    the Creator of the ends of the earth.
He does not faint or grow weary,
    his understanding is unsearchable.
He gives power to the faint,
    and to him who has no might he increases strength.
Even youths shall faint and be weary,
    and young men shall fall exhausted;
but they who wait for the Lord shall renew
      their strength,
    they shall mount up with wings like eagles,
    they shall run and not be weary,
    they shall walk and not faint.

Isaiah 40:28–31

98   When you pass through the waters I will be with you;
    and through the rivers, they shall not overwhelm
      you;

when you walk through fire you shall not be burned,
    and the flame shall not consume you.
For I am the Lord your God,
    the Holy One of Israel, your Savior.

Isaiah 43:2–3a

99   How beautiful upon the mountains are the feet
    of him who brings good tidings,
who publishes peace, who brings good tidings of good,
    who publishes salvation,
    who says to Zion, "Your God reigns."

Isaiah 52:7

100   Seek the Lord while he may be found,
    call upon him while he is near;
let the wicked forsake his way,
    and the unrighteous man his thoughts;
let him return to the Lord, that he may
    have mercy on him,
and to our God, for he will abundantly pardon.

Isaiah 55:6–7

101   Thus says the Lord:
"Keep justice, and do righteousness,
    for soon my salvation will come,
    and my deliverance be revealed.
Blessed is the man who does this,
    and the son of man who holds it fast,
who keeps the sabbath, not profaning it,
    and keeps his hand from doing any evil."

Isaiah 56:1–2

102   For thus says the high and lofty One
    who inhabits eternity, whose name is Holy:
"I dwell in the high and holy place,
    and also with him who is of a contrite and
        humble spirit,
    to revive the spirit of the humble,
    and to revive the heart of the contrite."

Isaiah 57:15

103   The Spirit of the Lord God is upon me,
        because the Lord has anointed me
        to bring good tidings to the afflicted;
    he has sent me to bind up the brokenhearted,
        to proclaim liberty to the captives,
        and the opening of the prison to those who are
            bound;
    to proclaim the year of the Lord's favor,
        and the day of vengeance of our God;
    to comfort all who mourn;
    to grant to those who mourn in Zion—
        to give them a garland instead of ashes,
        the oil of gladness instead of mourning,
        the mantle of praise instead of a faint spirit;
    that they may be called oaks of righteousness,
        the planting of the Lord, that he may be glorified.
                              Isaiah 61:1–3

104   Thus says the Lord: "Let not the wise man glory in his wisdom, let not the mighty man glory in his might, let not the rich man glory in his riches; but let him who glories glory in this, that he understands and knows me, that I am the Lord who practice kindness, justice, and righteousness in the earth; for in these things I delight, says the Lord."
                              Jeremiah 9:23–24

105   I know the plans I have for you, says the Lord, plans for welfare and not for evil, to give you a future and a hope. Then you will call upon me and come and pray to me, and I will hear you. You will seek me and find me; when you seek me with all your heart.
                              Jeremiah 29:11–13

106   The steadfast love of the Lord never ceases,
        his mercies never come to an end;
    they are new every morning;
        great is thy faithfulness.
    The Lord is my portion, says my soul,
        therefore I will hope in him.
                            Lamentations 3:22–24

107　The Lord is good to those who wait for him,
　　　　to the soul that seeks him.
　　It is good that one should wait quietly
　　　　for the salvation of the Lord.

Lamentations 3:25–26

108　Let us test and examine our ways,
　　　　and return to the Lord!
　　Let us lift up our hearts and hands
　　　　to God in heaven.

Lamentations 3:40–41

109　"Yet even now," says the Lord,
　　　　"return to me with all your heart,
　　with fasting, with weeping, and with mourning;
　　　　and rend your hearts and not your garments."
　　Return to the Lord, your God,
　　　　for he is gracious and merciful,
　　slow to anger, and abounding in steadfast love.

Joel 2:12–13

110　Many nations shall come, and say:
　　"Come, let us go up to the mountain of the Lord,
　　　　to the house of the God of Jacob;
　　that he may teach us his ways
　　　　and we may walk in his paths."
　　For out of Zion shall go forth the law,
　　　　and the word of the Lord from Jerusalem.

Micah 4:2

111　With what shall I come before the Lord,
　　　　and bow myself before God on high?
　　He has showed you, O man, what is good;
　　　　and what does the Lord require of you
　　　　but to do justice, and to love kindness,
　　　　and to walk humbly with your God?

Micah 6:6a, 8

112　The Lord is in his holy temple;
　　　　let all the earth keep silence before him.

Habakkuk 2:20

113   Sing and rejoice, O daughter of Zion; for lo I come and I will dwell in the midst of you, says the Lord.

Zechariah 2:10

114   These are the things that you shall do: Speak the truth to one another, render in your gates judgments that are true and make for peace, do not devise evil in your hearts against one another, and love no false oath, for all these things I hate, says the Lord.

Zechariah 8:16–17

115   Rejoice greatly, O daughter of Zion!
      Shout aloud, O daughter of Jerusalem!
Lo, your king comes to you;
      triumphant and victorious is he,
humble and riding on an ass,
      on a colt the foal of an ass.
I will cut off the chariot from Ephraim
      and the war horse from Jerusalem;
and the battle bow shall be cut off,
      and he shall command peace to the nations;
his dominion shall be from sea to sea,
      and from the River to the ends of the earth.

Zechariah 9:9–10

B.   FROM THE NEW TESTAMENT

116   It is written, "Man shall not live by bread alone, but by every word that proceeds from the mouth of God."

Matthew 4:4

117   Jesus said, ". . . it is written, 'You shall worship the Lord your God and him only shall you serve.'"

Matthew 4:10

118   Jesus said, "Blessed are the peacemakers, for they shall be called sons of God."

Matthew 5:9

119   Jesus said, "You have heard that it was said, 'You shall love your neighbor and hate your enemy.' But I say to you, love your enemies and pray for those who persecute

you, so that you may be sons of your Father who is in heaven; for he makes his sun rise on the evil and on the good, and sends rain on the just and on the unjust."

Matthew 5:43–45

120   Ask, and it will be given you; seek, and you will find; knock, and it will be opened to you. For every one who asks receives, and he who seeks finds, and to him who knocks it will be opened.

Matthew 7:7–8

121   Jesus said: "Whatever you wish that men would do to you, do so to them; for this is the law and the prophets."

Matthew 7:12

122   Enter by the narrow gate; for the gate is wide and the way is easy, that leads to destruction, and those who enter by it are many. For the gate is narrow and the way is hard, that leads to life, and those who find it are few.

Matthew 7:13–14

123   Jesus said, "Not every one who says to me, 'Lord, Lord,' shall enter the kingdom of heaven, but he who does the will of my Father who is in heaven."

Matthew 7:21

124   Jesus said: "Come to me, all who labor and are heavy-laden, and I will give you rest. Take my yoke upon you, and learn from me; for I am gentle and lowly in heart, and you will find rest for your souls. For my yoke is easy, and my burden is light."

Matthew 11:28–30

125   Jesus told his disciples, "If any man would come after me, let him deny himself and take up his cross and follow me. For whoever would save his life will lose it, and whoever loses his life for my sake will find it. For what will it profit a man if he gains the whole world and forfeits his life?"

Matthew 16:24–26

126   Jesus said, "Again I say to you, if two of you agree on earth about anything they ask, it will be done for them by my Father in heaven. For where two or three are gathered in my name, there am I in the midst of them."

Matthew 18:19–20

127 Behold, I bring you good news of a great joy which will come to all the people; for to you is born this day in the city of David a Savior, who is Christ the Lord.

Luke 2:10–11

128 For God so loved the world that he gave his only Son, that whoever believes in him should not perish but have eternal life.

John 3:16

129 The hour is coming, and now is, when the true worshipers will worship the Father in spirit and truth, for such the Father seeks to worship him. God is spirit, and those who worship him must worship in spirit and truth.

John 4:23–24

130 Jesus said, "I am the resurrection and the life; he who believes in me, though he die, yet shall he live, and whoever lives and believes in me shall never die. Do you believe this?"

John 11:25–26

131 Greater love has no man than this, that a man lay down his life for his friends. You are my friends if you do what I command you. No longer do I call you servants, for the servant does not know what his master is doing; but I have called you friends, for all that I have heard from my Father I have made known to you.

John 15:13–15

132 Truly I perceive that God shows no partiality, but in every nation any one who fears him and does what is right is acceptable to him.

Acts 10:34–35

133 O the depth of the riches and wisdom and knowledge of God! How unsearchable are his judgments and how inscrutable his ways! "For who has known the mind of the Lord, or who has been his counselor? Or who has given a gift to him that he might be repaid?" For from him and through him and to him are all things. To him be glory for ever. Amen.

Romans 11:33–36

134   Do not be conformed to this world but be transformed by the renewal of your mind, that you may prove what is the will of God, what is good and acceptable and perfect.

Romans 12:2

135   Besides this you know what hour it is, how it is full time now for you to wake from sleep. For salvation is nearer to us now than when we first believed; the night is far gone, the day is at hand. Let us then cast off the works of darkness and put on the armor of light.

Romans 13:11–12

136   None of us lives to himself, and none of us dies to himself. If we live, we live to the Lord, and if we die, we die to the Lord; so then whether we live or whether we die we are the Lord's. For to this end Christ died and lived again, that he might be Lord both of the dead and of the living.

Romans 14:7–9

137   For we are fellow workmen for God; you are God's field, God's building. According to the commission of God given to me, like a skilled master builder I laid a foundation, and another man is building upon it. Let each man take care how he builds upon it. For no other foundation can any one lay than that which is laid, which is Jesus Christ.

I Corinthians 3:9–11

138   Do you not know that you are God's temple and that God's Spirit dwells in you? If any one destroys God's temple, God will destroy him. For God's temple is holy, and that temple you are.

I Corinthians 3:16–17

139   The Lord is the Spirit, and where the Spirit of the Lord is, there is freedom.

II Corinthians 3:17

140   We are ambassadors for Christ, God making his appeal through us. We beseech you on behalf of Christ, be reconciled to God.

II Corinthians 5:20

141   Grace to you and peace from God the Father and our Lord Jesus Christ, who gave himself for our sins to deliver us from the present evil age, according to the will of our God and Father; to whom be the glory for ever and ever. Amen.

Galatians 1:3–5

142   You were called to freedom, brethren; only do not use your freedom as an opportunity for the flesh, but through love be servants of one another. For the whole law is fulfilled in one word, "You shall love your neighbor as yourself."

Galatians 5:13–14

143   Brethren, if a man is overtaken in any trespass, you who are spiritual should restore him in a spirit of gentleness. Look to yourself, lest you too be tempted. Bear one another's burdens, and so fulfil the law of Christ.

Galatians 6:1–2

144   Let us not grow weary in well-doing, for in due season we shall reap, if we do not lose heart. So then, as we have opportunity, let us do good to all men, and especially to those who are of the household of faith.

Galatians 6:9–10

145   Blessed be the God and Father of our Lord Jesus Christ, who has blessed us in Christ with every spiritual blessing in the heavenly places, even as he chose us in him before the foundation of the world, that we should be holy and blameless before him.

Ephesians 1:3–4

146   He has made known to us in all wisdom and insight the mystery of his will, according to his purpose which he set forth in Christ as a plan for the fulness of time, to unite all things in him, things in heaven and things on earth.

Ephesians 1:9–10

147   I . . . beg you to lead a life worthy of the calling to which you have been called, with all lowliness and meekness, with patience, forbearing one another in love, eager to maintain the unity of the Spirit in the bond of peace.

Ephesians 4:1–3

148   Let all bitterness and wrath and anger and clamor and slander be put away from you, with all malice, and be kind to one another, tenderhearted, forgiving one another, as God in Christ forgave you.

Ephesians 4:31–32

149   Be strong in the Lord and in the strength of his might. Put on the whole armor of God, that you may be able to stand against the wiles of the devil. For we are not contending against flesh and blood, but against the principalities, against the powers, against the world rulers of this present darkness, against the spiritual hosts of wickedness in the heavenly places. Therefore take the whole armor of God, that you may be able to withstand in the evil day, and having done all, to stand.

Ephesians 6:10–13

150   Do nothing from selfishness or conceit, but in humility count others better than yourselves. Let each of you look not only to his own interests, but also the interests of others. Have this mind among yourselves, which you have in Christ Jesus.

Philippians 2:3–5

151   And being found in human form he humbled himself and became obedient unto death, even death on a cross. Therefore God has highly exalted him and bestowed on him the name which is above every name, that at the name of Jesus every knee should bow, in heaven and on earth and under the earth, and every tongue confess that Jesus Christ is Lord, to the glory of God the Father.

Philippians 2:8–11

152   Rejoice in the Lord always; again I will say, Rejoice. Let all men know your forbearance.

Philippians 4:4–5

153   Have no anxiety about anything, but in everything by prayer and supplication with thanksgiving let your requests be made known to God. And the peace of God, which passes all understanding, will keep your hearts and your minds in Christ Jesus.

Philippians 4:6–7

154   Finally, brethren, whatever is true, whatever is honorable, whatever is just, whatever is pure, whatever is lovely, whatever is gracious, if there is any excellence, if there is anything worthy of praise, think about these things. What you have learned and received and heard and seen in me, do; and the God of peace will be with you.

Philippians 4:8–9

155   Put on then, as God's chosen ones, holy and beloved, compassion, kindness, lowliness, meekness, and patience, forbearing one another and, if one has a complaint against another, forgiving each other; as the Lord has forgiven you, so you also must forgive. And above all these put on love, which binds everything together in perfect harmony. And let the peace of Christ rule in your hearts.

Colossians 3:12–15

156   Whatever your task, work heartily, as serving the Lord and not men, knowing that from the Lord you will receive the inheritance as your reward; you are serving the Lord Christ.

Colossians 3:23–24

157   Do your best to present yourself to God as one approved, a workman who has no need to be ashamed, rightly handling the word of truth.

II Timothy 2:15

158   For the grace of God has appeared for the salvation of all men, training us to renounce irreligion and worldly passions, and to live sober, upright, and godly lives in this world, awaiting our blessed hope, the appearing of the glory of our great God and savior Jesus Christ, who gave himself for us to redeem us from all iniquity and to purify for himself a people of his own who are zealous for good deeds.

Titus 2:11–14

159   Since then we have a great high priest who has passed through the heavens, Jesus, the Son of God, let us hold fast our confession. For we have not a high priest who is unable to sympathize with our weaknesses, but one who in every respect has been tempted as we are, yet without sin-

ning. Let us then with confidence draw near to the throne of grace, that we may receive mercy and find grace to help in time of need.

Hebrews 4:14–16

160   Therefore, since we are surrounded by so great a cloud of witnesses, let us also lay aside every weight, and sin which clings so closely, and let us run with perseverance the race that is set before us, looking to Jesus the pioneer and perfecter of our faith, who for the joy that was set before him endured the cross, despising the shame, and is seated at the right hand of the throne of God.

Hebrews 12:1–2

161   Be ye doers of the word, and not hearers only.

James 1:22

162   Religion that is pure and undefiled before God and the Father is this: to visit orphans and widows in their affliction, and to keep oneself unstained from the world.

James 1:27

163   Draw near to God and he will draw near to you.

James 4:8

164   He that would love life and see good days,
let him keep his tongue from evil
and his lips from speaking guile;
let him turn away from evil and do right;
let him seek peace and pursue it.

I Peter 3:10–11

165   And after you have suffered a little while, the God of all grace, who has called you to his eternal glory in Christ, will himself restore, establish, and strengthen you. To him be the dominion for ever and ever. Amen.

I Peter 5:10–11

166   If we say we have no sin, we deceive ourselves, and the truth is not in us. If we confess our sins, he is faithful and just, and will forgive our sins and cleanse us from all unrighteousness.

I John 1:8–9

167 See what love the Father has given us, that we should be called children of God; and so we are. The reason why the world does not know us is that it did not know him. Beloved, we are God's children now; it does not yet appear what we shall be, but we know that when he appears we shall be like him, for we shall see him as he is.

I John 3:1–2

168 Beloved, let us love one another; for love is of God, and he who loves is born of God and knows God.

I John 4:7

169 There is no fear in love, but perfect love casts out fear. For fear has to do with punishment, and he who fears is not perfected in love. We love, because he first loved us.

I John 4:18–19

170 If any one says, "I love God," and hates his brother, he is a liar; for he who does not love his brother whom he has seen, cannot love God whom he has not seen. And this commandment we have from him, that he who loves God should love his brother also.

I John 4:20–21

171 Grace to you and peace from him who is and who was and who is to come, and from the seven spirits who are before his throne, and from Jesus Christ the faithful witness, the first-born of the dead, and the ruler of kings on earth. To him who loves us and has freed us from our sins by his blood and made us a kingdom, priests to his God and Father, to him be glory and dominion for ever and ever. Amen.

Revelation 1:4–6

172 Behold, I stand at the door and knock; if any one hears my voice and opens the door, I will come in to him and eat with him, and he with me.

Revelation 3:20

173 Worthy art thou, our Lord and God,
  to receive glory and honor and power,
  for thou didst create all things,
  and by thy will they existed and were created.

Revelation 4:11

174 Blessing and glory and wisdom and thanksgiving and honor and power and might be to our God for ever and ever! Amen.

Revelation 7:12

175 Behold, the dwelling of God is with men. He will dwell with them, and they shall be his people, and God himself will be with them.

Revelation 21:3

C. FROM OTHER SOURCES

176 Look at the generations of old, and see; did ever any trust in the Lord, and was confounded? Or did any abide in his fear and was forsaken? Or whom did he ever despise, that called upon him? For the Lord is full of compassion and mercy, long-suffering, and very pitiful, and forgiveth sins, and saveth in time of affliction.

Ecclesiasticus 2:10–11

177 Let thy mind be upon the ordinances of the Lord, and meditate continually in his commandments; he shall establish thine heart and give thee wisdom at thine own desire.

Ecclesiasticus 6:37

178 Dearly beloved, we have come apart into this house of prayer and praise to renew our souls at the fountain of life. We are all children of the household of faith, fellow-travellers toward his promised rest. With humble hearts and hopeful spirits let us offer up our prayers to him who, though he dwelleth on high, is yet very present and never faileth to listen to all who call upon him out of their need and hope and love.

The Pilgrim Hymnal

179 Ye who are gathered in this place submit yourselves to the will and loving direction of God that in this hour of worship you miss no good made ready for your souls. Devotedly listen to the message of grace and utter your need to His listening ear. He shall surely guide you to the better life and thus bring you at last to your eternal home.

180 Glory be to the Father, and to the Son, and to the
Holy Ghost, as it was in the beginning, is now and ever shall
be, world without end. Amen.

Gloria Patri, 2nd Century

181 We praise Thee, O God:
> We acknowledge Thee to be the Lord,
> All the earth doth worship Thee, the Father everlast-
>   ing.
> To Thee all angels cry aloud; the heavens and all the
>   powers therein.
> To Thee cherubim and seraphim continually do cry:
> Holy, Holy, Holy, Lord God of Sabaoth.
> Heaven and earth are full of the majesty of Thy glory.

Te Deum, 4th Century

182 Dearly beloved, in the holy quiet of this hour, let us
draw nigh to him who heareth prayer; let us remember that
he listeneth more to our hearts than to our words, and that
we are the children of his love. As we bow before him may
we be delivered from blindness and prejudice and from fear.
May the God of all grace so cleanse our hearts and so order
our minds that they shall be open to the kindly touch of the
mysterious Spirit of him before whom we wait.

The Pilgrim Hymnal

183 On this day, appointed for rest and spiritual quickening, we humbly approach Thee and thank Thee for so precious a gift. Each week this herald of peace comes to us with
the message ever new, giving strength to the weary, relief to
the burdened, and cheer to the faint of heart. It reminds us
that Thy protecting hand is over us at all times, from the
beginning even unto the end of our life; that it is Thou
who blessest our work and helpest us to acquire the things
we need for our sustenance.

Union Prayer Book

184 Blessed art Thou, O Lord,
> Who hast given unto man the insight of knowledge,
> to understand Thy wonders,
> (to discern Thy truth,)
> to tell forth Thine abundant mercies.

Blessed art Thou, O God of compassion and grace,
for the greatness of (Thy) power,
the abundance of Thy truth
the profusion of Thy mercies
over all Thy works.

The Dead Sea Scriptures

185 Ye people now
In reverence bow,
In Holy fear draw nigh,
Nor heedlessly invoke the Lord most high.
With joy and exultation
Lift up your hearts in praise;
With awe and adoration
In song your voices raise.
His boundless love declare,
His power proclaim abroad,
Let all men everywhere
Exalt the Lord our God!

from *Parsifal*, 1882

186 God does not sound trumpets before.
He comes as silent as a mist.
One does not hear him at the door,
To enter he does not insist.
But if the door is open wide
So gladly will he come inside.

187 Father, in thy mysterious presence kneeling,
Fain would our souls feel all thy kindling love;
For we are weak, and need some deep revealing
Of Truth and strength and calmness from above.

Samuel Johnson, 1822–1882

188 It is Sunday! It is Sunday! Get awake! Don't sit down!
Come to this good thing which won't come to you unless you
come to it. Come to meeting, everybody! Come all! Don't sit
in your town today. The words of God have arrived! Come
get them. No one else can get them for you. You must come!
Sunday! Sunday!

The Cameroons

189   The Lord is in his holy temple;
    Let all the earth keep silence before him.
    And heart, keep thou silence;
    Gather up thy wandering thoughts,
    Thy vain imaginings;
    Hold thyself open to the mystic power
    Just for this little hour.
    Let all the vexing cares,
    Thy roving thoughts
    Keep silence in his holy temple
    Where thy spirit now has entered.
    To worship the most High.

Jeanne Hatch Mickie

190   He bids us open wide our hearts to receive his blessing, and to be at home in this fellowship. For we
are of God's one family in the whole wide earth.
At this hour when we are met in fellowship, Christians
around the world are meeting, in their own ways.
Mighty tides of prayer are rising.
Let us lift our hearts to worship the God, the Father
of all, in spirit and in truth, in fellowship and in
love.

Resources For Worship

191   Let none who are here present remain mere critics or
spectators. Let us all be communicants in the moral life of
this meeting, entering into its devotion with a spirit of com-
radeship, with a becoming sense of our several needs, and
with reverence for the ideal of human character.

Stanton Coit

192   We are met in fellowship in this holy meeting-place.
    This is God's house.
    This is none other than the gate of heaven.
    Need we implore his presence with us?
    Nay! Rather, we are his guests.

193   Praise to the Lord, the Almighty, the King of Creation!
    Praise Him, for He is thy health and salvation.
    All ye who hear,

Now to this altar draw near,
Joining in glad adoration.

Joachim Neander, 1650–1680

194 Dear Brethren, we are met at the command and by
the invitation of God to worship him, to offer the sacrifice
of praise and thanksgiving, to hear and meditate upon his
holy Word, and to seek at his hand the blessings which he is
waiting to bestow. Let us, therefore, draw near with reverence and godly fear, laying aside all insincerity and thought-
lessness, that we may seek the face of God our Father, and
hear his voice, and offer unto him that surrender of ourselves which is our spiritual worship.

In the name of the Father, the Son, and the Holy Spirit
we meet together, a Church of the living God.

Directory for Public Worship

195 Dearly beloved, God, in whom we live and move and
have our being, never leaves us, day or night. But the very
nearness and custom of his presence hide him from our in-
firm and sinful hearts; and under cover of this darkness our
inner discernment becomes dim, temptations gain shame-
ful power, and the good that is in us droops and fades. To
clear such blindness away and recover the pure wisdom of
a Christian mind, we are called to this day of remembrance
and this house of prayer. Entering here, therefore, we cross
the threshold of eternal things and commune with the
Father who seeth in secret. Let us shake off the dust of
transitory care and every disguise that can come between us
and God, and remembering whose disciples we are, come
to the simplicity, though it should be also to the sorrow of
Christ.

James Martineau, 1805–1900

196 The love of Christ has gathered us together.

Let us rejoice in him and be glad. By this shall all men
know that we are his disciples, if we have love one for another.

The Feast of St. Bartholomew

197   Joyful, Joyful, we adore thee
God of glory, Lord of love;
Hearts unfold like flowers before thee,
Opening to the sun above.
All thy works with joy surround thee,
Earth and heaven reflect thy rays.
Stars and angels sing around thee.
Center of unbroken praise.
    Now to thee, the King, eternal, immortal,
invisible, the only God, be honor and glory,
world without end. Amen.

Henry Van Dyke, 1886–1933

198   Wrapt in the sacred stillness of this sanctuary and
filled with the consciousness of God's presence, we turn
away from the things of earth to contemplate the mysterious
nature of our inner being and to capture and to hold the
heavenly vision revealed to our soul. We know that not with
eyes of flesh nor with power of mind can we see and grasp
the sublime truths of eternity . . . We are face to face with
God . . . No longer do we feel alone in the world of struggle and strife . . . God is ever near to us, strengthening
us in our weakness and directing our will to earnest effort
and high endeavor. . . . Surely God is in this place.

Union Prayer Book

199   Let us adore the ever-living God, and render praise
unto Him who spread out the heavens and established the
earth, whose glory is revealed in the heavens above and
whose greatness is manifest through the world. He is our
God; there is none else.

Union Prayer Book

200   Lo, God, is here! Let us adore
And own how solemn is this place!
So all within us feel his power,
And silent bow before his face;
Who know his power, his grace to prove,
Serve him with awe, with reverence, love.

John Wesley, 1703–1791

201   May his (God's) name be magnified and hallowed in the world, which he has made according to his will, and may his kingly role be established in your lifetime . . . May the name of the Lord be praised from now on and forever. May the prayer and petition of all (Israel) find acceptance before our Father who is in heaven.

> May his great name be blessed,
> Forever and to all eternity.

The Kaddish

202   Extolled and hallowed be the name of God throughout the world which He has created according to His will. And may He speedily establish His kingdom of righteousness on earth.

Union Prayer Book

203   Observe good faith and justice toward all nations; cultivate peace and harmony with all. It will be worthy of a free, enlightened, and great nation, to give to mankind the example of a people always guided by an exalted justice and benevolence.

George Washington, 1732–1799

204   With malice towards none, with charity for all, with firmness in the right as God gives us to see the right, let us strive on to finish the work we are in, and to do all which may achieve and cherish a just and lasting peace among ourselves and with all nations.

Abraham Lincoln, 1809–1865

205   Now let the heavens be joyful,
> Let earth her song begin;
> Let the round world keep triumph,
> And all that is therein;
> Invisible and visible,
> Their notes let all things blend,
> For Christ the Lord is risen,
> Our joy that hath no end.

St. John of Damascus, 700–754

206   Beloved, let us love: love is of God;
        In God alone hath love its true abode.

        Beloved, let us love: for they who love,
        They only, are His sons, born from above.

        Beloved, let us love: for love is rest,
        And he who loveth not abides unblest.

        Beloved, let us love: for love is light,
        And he who loveth not dwelleth in night.

        Beloved, let us love: for only this
        Shall we behold that God who loved us.

                         Horatius Bonar, 1808–1889

207   I say to all men, far and near
        That He is risen today:
        That He is with us now and here,
        And evermore shall stay.

        And what I say, let each this morn
        Go tell it to his friend,
        That soon in every place shall dawn
        His kingdom without end.

                     George F. D. von Hardenberg, 1802

208   This is the house of God. It is consecrated unto His worship. For those who seek its shelter the calm restfulness of its holy atmosphere refreshes the soul. There comes to us here a keener consciousness of our God, a fuller and freer recognition of His presence and His power in all the experiences of our life . . . Too often do we go our way day after day and forget His wisdom and guidance. The tasks and trials, the pursuits and pleasures of daily life absorb us and crowd the thought of God from our hearts.

    Therefore the Sabbath is given us. It is as a gentle voice bidding us turn for a moment from our daily toil, that we may refresh ourselves with the waters of life drawn from the wells of salvation.

                               Union Prayer Book

209   Beloved, we are come together in the presence of Almighty God and of the whole company of heaven to offer unto him through our Lord Jesus Christ our worship and praise and thanksgiving; to make confession of our sins; to

pray, as well for others as for ourselves, that we may know more truly the greatness of God's love and show forth in our lives the fruits of his grace; and to ask on behalf of all men such things as their well-being doth require.

A Book of Services and Prayers

210 We are taught in the Holy Scriptures not to forsake the assembling of ourselves together, to meet with God and learn from him.

Wherefore I say to each one of you: Thy Lord is here to meet thee. Remove now earthly thoughts from thy mind for the place whereon thou standest is holy ground.

Let thy praise be from thy heart, and do not in thy praying mock the Lord with idle thoughts or empty speech. Read reverently his holy Word, and do thy part to understand the message he may send.

And to this end, I pray you every one to ask his grace and help—first, for yourselves, that you may fix your minds on him; and then for us all, that, thus praying for one another, we may be greatly blest.

A Book of Services and Prayers

211 Minister and People:

> Holy, holy, holy, Lord God Almighty, which was, and is, and is to come.

Minister:

> Great and marvelous are thy works, Lord God Almighty
> Just and true, are thy ways, thou King of Ages;
> Worthy art thou, O Lord, to receive glory and honor and power;
> For thou hast revealed all things, and because thou hast taken unto thee thy great power and hast reigned.
> Worthy is the Lamb that was slain, to receive power and wisdom, strength and honor and glory and blessing, and he shall reign forever and ever.

Minister and People:

> Blessing, and glory, and thanksgiving, and honor, and power, and might, be unto our God forever and ever. Amen.

Book of Common Worship

212 Dearly beloved, we are assembled and met together;
to render thanks to Almighty God, our heavenly Father, for the great benefits that we have received at his hands;

to set forth his most worthy praise;

to acknowledge and confess our sins;

to hear his most holy word;

and to ask those things which are requisite and necessary, as well for the body as the soul.

Let us, therefore, draw near to God with a humble, lowly, penitent, and obedient heart; to the end that we may obtain forgiveness and grace, and adore him for his infinite goodness and mercy.

A Book of Services and Prayers

213 Come to this reverent place where prayer
Flows from the heart, where music breaks
The hardened mood, and everywhere
The glowing light of day remakes
Our shadowed life. Come, hear again
The voices of long ago,
How over all the cries of men
The mighty word of Him we know
As Master bids us follow near.

Come, fill your minds with thoughts as new
As life, and old as God, and hear
His truth and find His way, that through
Our common need we know the lift
Of Life to common good, begun
And ended in the priceless gift
Of Him whose truths shine as the sun.
The Lord is in this holy place.
Lift up your hearts, that we may praise
His name, until we know the grace
And power He gives for all our days.

Herbert Henry Hines

214 We have come together to worship God:
to thank him for his goodness, and to praise him for his glory;
to confess our sins, and to hear his Word;

to ask his blessing, for ourselves and others.
We come to meditate on things unseen, and to draw
strength from things eternal:
to seek courage for our duty, and guidance for our
way;
to remember that God made us, and that we find
our life in him.

A Book of Services and Prayers

215 Love built this shrine; these hallowed walls uprose
To give seclusion from the hurrying throng,
From tumult of the street, complaint and wrong,
From rivalry and strife, from taunt of foes—
If foes thou hast. On silent feet come in,
Bow low in penitence. Whoe'er thou art
Thou, too, hast sinned. Uplift in prayer thy heart.
Thy Father's blessing waiteth. Read within
This holy place, in pictured light portrayed,
The characters of worthies who, from years
Long past, still speak the message here displayed
In universal language not to fade.
Leave then thy burden, all thy cares and fears;
Faith, hope, and love are thine, for thou hast prayed.

John Davidson, 1857–1909

216 We come in the name of the Lord Jesus:
who went, as his custom was, into the synagogue
on the sabbath day;
who taught us to pray;
who promised his presence to the two or three; his
rest to the heavy-laden; and his peace to all who
love and trust him.
Let us, therefore, turn to him in prayer, who is not
far from any one of us.

A Book of Services and Prayers

217 Blessed be the name of God for ever and ever; for
wisdom and might are His. He giveth wisdom to the wise
and knowledge to them that know understanding. Every
good gift is from above, coming down from the Father of
light. Praise ye the Lord.

Devotional Services

D. ASCRIPTIONS OF PRAISE

218 O Lord, our Lord,
      how majestic is thy name in all the earth!
      Thou whose glory above the heavens is chanted
      by the mouth of babes and infants,
      thou hast founded a bulwark because of thy foes,
      to still the enemy and the avenger.
      O Lord, our Lord,
      how majestic is thy name in all the earth!

Psalms 8:1–2, 9

219 Let the words of my mouth and the
          meditation of my heart
      be acceptable in thy sight,
      O Lord, my rock and my redeemer.

Psalms 19:14

220 O Lord, I love the habitation of thy house,
      and the place where thy glory dwells.

Psalms 26:8

221 Have mercy on me, O God, according to thy steadfast
          love;
      according to thy abundant mercy blot out my trans-
          gressions.
      Wash me thoroughly from my iniquity,
          and cleanse me from my sin!

Psalms 51:1–2

222 Create in me a clean heart, O God,
          and put a new and right spirit within me.
      Cast me not away from thy presence,
          and take not thy holy Spirit from me.

Psalms 51:10–11

223 O Lord, open thou my lips,
          and my mouth shall show forth thy praise.

Psalms 51:15

224   Be merciful to me, O God,
        be merciful to me,
        for in thee my soul takes refuge;
    in the shadow of thy wings I will take refuge,
        till the storms of destruction pass by. . . .
    God will send forth his steadfast love and his faithfulness.

                                      Psalms 57:1, 3

225   I will give thanks to thee, O Lord, among the peoples;
    I will sing praises to thee among the nations.
    For thy steadfast love is great to the heavens,
        thy faithfulness to the clouds.
    Be exalted, O God, above the heavens!
        Let thy glory be over all the earth!

                                      Psalms 57:9–11

226   Whom have I in heaven but thee?
        And there is nothing upon earth that
            I desire besides thee.
    My flesh and my heart may fail,
        but God is the strength of my heart
        and my portion for ever.

                                      Psalms 73:25–26

227   There is none like thee among the gods, O Lord,
        nor are there any works like thine.
    All the nations thou hast made shall come
        and bow down before thee, O Lord,
        and shall glorify thy name.
    For thou art great and doest wondrous things,
    thou alone art God.

                                      Psalms 86:8–10

228   Lord, thou hast been our dwelling place
        in all generations.
    Before the mountains were brought forth,
        or ever thou hadst formed the earth and the world,
        from everlasting to everlasting thou art God.

                                      Psalms 90:1–2

229   Of old thou didst lay the foundation of the earth,
      and the heavens are the work of thy hands.
  They will perish, but thou dost endure;
      they will all wear out like a garment.
  Thou changest them like raiment, and they pass away;
      but thou art the same, and thy years have no end.
                        Psalms 102:25–27

230   O Lord, thou hast searched me and known me!
  Thou knowest when I sit down and when I rise up;
      thou discernest my thoughts from afar.
  Thou searchest out my path and my lying down,
      and art acquainted with all my ways.
                        Psalms 139:1–3

231   Search me, O God, and know my heart!
      Try me and know my thoughts!
  And see if there be any wicked way in me,
      and lead me in the way everlasting.
                        Psalms 139:23–24

232   Blessed be the name of God for ever and ever,
      to whom belong wisdom and might.
  He changes times and seasons;
      he removes kings and sets up kings;
  he gives wisdom to the wise
      and knowledge to those who have understanding;
  he reveals deep and mysterious things;
      he knows what is in the darkness,
      and the light dwells with him.
  To thee, O God of my fathers,
      I give thanks and praise,
  for thou hast given me wisdom and strength
  and hast now made known to me
      what we asked of thee.
                        Daniel 2:20–23

233   Now to him who by the power at work within us is able to do far more abundantly than all that we ask or think, to him be glory in the church and in Christ Jesus to all generations, for ever and ever.
                        Ephesians 3:20–21

234   Blessed be the God and Father of our Lord Jesus Christ! By his great mercy we have been born anew to a living hope through the resurrection of Jesus Christ from the dead, and to an inheritance which is imperishable, undefiled, and unfading, kept in heaven for you.

I Peter 1:3–4

235   To him who loves us and has freed us from our sins by his blood and made us a kingdom, priests to his God and Father, to him be glory and dominion for ever and ever. Amen.

Revelation 1:5–6

236   And I heard every creature in heaven and on earth and under the earth and in the sea, and all therein, saying, "To him who sits upon the throne and to the Lamb be blessing and honor and glory and might for ever and ever!"

Revelation 5:13

237   Thou art, O God, the life and light
  Of all this wondrous world we see;
 Its glow by day, its smile by night,
  Are but reflections caught from Thee.
 Where'er we turn, Thy glories shine,
 And all things fair and bright are Thine.

Thomas Moore, 1779–1852

238   Great art Thou, O Lord, and greatly to be praised;
 Great is Thy power, and of Thy wisdom there is no end.
 And man, being part of Thy creation, desires to praise
  Thee, —
 Man, who bears about with him his mortality,
 The witness of his sin, even the witness that Thou
  "resistest the proud," —
 Yet man, this part of Thy creation, desires to praise
  Thee.
 Thou movest us to delight in praising Thee;
 For Thou hast formed us for Thyself,
 And our hearts are restless till they find rest in
  Thee.

St. Augustine, 354–430

239   O God of love, whose spirit wakes
       In every human breast
   Whom love, and love alone can know,
       In whom all hearts find rest,
   Help us to spread
       Thy gracious reign
       Till greed and hate shall cease,
   And kindness dwell in human hearts,
   And all the earth find peace.

Henry Hallan Tweedy, 1868–1953

240   Lord, I love the habitation of thy house, and the place where thy glory dwelleth. As for me, I will worship and bow down: I will bend the knee before the Lord, my Maker. And as for me, may my prayer unto thee, O Lord, be in an acceptable time: O God, in the abundance of thy loving kindness answer me in the truth of thy salvation.

Union Prayer Book

241   We praise Thee, O God, our Redeemer, Creator
   In grateful devotion our tribute we bring.
   We lay it before Thee, we kneel and adore Thee,
   We bless Thy holy Name, glad praises we sing.

   With voices united our praises we offer,
   And gladly our anthems of worship we raise.
   Thy strong arm will guide us, our God is beside us,
   To Thee, our great Redeemer, for ever be praise.

Julia Bulkley Cady Cory, 1902

242   Blessed be thou, O Lord our God and God of our fathers; God of Abraham, Isaac and Jacob, a mighty and faithful God, a most high God, Creator of heaven and earth, our shield and shield of our fathers, our confidence in all generations. Blessed be thou, O God, the shield of Abraham.

   Holy and fearful is thy name and there is no God beside thee. Blessed be thou, O Lord, the holy God.

The Shemone Esreh

243   With Angels and Archangels, and with all the company of heaven, we laud and magnify thy glorious Name; evermore praising thee, and saying,

   HOLY, HOLY, HOLY, Lord God of hosts, Heaven and earth are full of thy glory: Glory be to thee, O Lord Most High. Amen.

The Book of Common Prayer

III

Invocations, Collects,
and
Prayers for the
Opening of Worship

A. FROM SCRIPTURE

1   O Lord God, thou art God, and thy words are true, and thou hast promised this good thing to thy servant; now therefore may it please thee to bless the house of thy servant, that it may continue for ever before thee; for thou O Lord God, hast spoken, and with thy blessing shall the house of thy servant be blessed for ever.

II Samuel 7:28–29

2   O Lord, our Lord,
> how majestic is thy name in all the earth!
Thou whose glory above the heavens is chanted.
When I look at thy heavens, the work of thy fingers
> the moon and the stars which thou hast established;
what is man that thou art mindful of him,
> and the son of man that thou dost care for him?
Yet thou hast made him little less than God,
> and dost crown him with glory and honor.
O Lord, our Lord,
> how majestic is thy name in all the earth!

Psalms 8:1, 3–5, 9

3   Keep back thy servant also from presumptuous sins;
> let them not have dominion over me!
Then I shall be blameless,
> and innocent of great transgression.
Let the words of my mouth and the meditation of my
> heart
> be acceptable in thy sight,
O Lord, my rock and my redeemer.

Psalms 19:13–14

4   Create in me a clean heart, O God
> and put a new and right spirit within me.
Cast me not away from thy presence,
> and take not thy holy Spirit from me.

Restore to me the joy of thy salvation,
and uphold me with a willing spirit.

Psalms 51:10–12

5 O Lord, open thou my lips,
and my mouth shall show forth thy praise.
For thou hast no delight in sacrifice;
were I to give a burnt offering, thou wouldst not be
pleased.
The sacrifice acceptable to God is a broken spirit;
a broken and contrite heart, O God, thou wilt not
despise.

Psalms 51:15–17

6 In thee, O Lord, do I take refuge;
let me never be put to shame!
In thy righteousness deliver me and rescue me;
incline thy ear to me, and save me!
Be thou to me a rock of refuge,
a strong fortress, to save me,
for thou art my rock and my fortress.

Psalms 71:1–3

7 Help us, O God of our salvation,
for the glory of thy name;
deliver us, and forgive our sins,
for thy name's sake!
Then we thy people, the flock of thy pasture,
will give thanks to thee for ever;
from generation to generation we will
recount thy praise.

Psalms 79:9, 13

8 How lovely is thy dwelling place, O Lord of Hosts!
My soul longs, yea, faints for the courts of the Lord;
Blessed are those who dwell in thy house,
ever singing thy praise!
O Lord God of hosts, hear my prayer;
give ear, O God of Jacob!
O Lord of hosts,
blessed is the man who trusts in thee!

Psalms 84:1–2, 4, 8, 12

9   Incline thy ear, O Lord, and answer me,
        for I am poor and needy.
    Preserve my life, for I am godly;
        save thy servant who trusts in thee.
    Thou art my God; be gracious to me, O Lord,
        for to thee do I cry all the day.
    Gladden the soul of thy servant,
        for to thee, O Lord, do I lift up my soul.
    For thou, O Lord, art good and forgiving,
        abounding in steadfast love to all who call on thee.
    Give ear, O Lord, to my prayer;
        hearken to my cry of supplication.

                                  Psalms 86:1–6

10   Lord, thou hast been our dwelling place in all
        generations.
    Before the mountains were brought forth,
        or ever thou hadst formed the earth and the world,
        from everlasting to everlasting thou art God.
    Satisfy us in the morning with thy steadfast love,
        that we may rejoice and be glad all our days.
    Make us glad as many days as thou hast afflicted us,
        and as many years as we have seen evil.
    Let thy work be manifest to thy servants,
        and thy glorious power to their children.
    Let the favor of the Lord our God be upon us,
        and establish thou the work of our hands upon us,
        yea, the work of our hands establish thou it.

                            Psalms 90:1–2, 14–17

11   Out of the depths I cry to thee, O Lord!
    Lord, hear my voice!
    Let thy ears be attentive to the voice of my supplications!
    If thou, O Lord, shouldst mark iniquities,
        Lord, who could stand?
    But there is forgiveness with thee,
        that thou mayest be feared.
    I wait for the Lord, my soul waits,
        and in his word I hope.

                            Psalms 130:1–5

B. FROM OTHER SOURCES

12   O God, the Father of our Lord and Saviour Jesus Christ, whose name is great, whose goodness is inexhaustible, thou God and Master of all things, who art blessed for ever. Sanctify, O Lord, our souls, bodies and spirits, and touch our apprehensions and minds, and search out our consciences, and cast out from us every evil thought, every base desire, all envy and pride and hypocrisy, all falsehood, all deceit, all worldly anxiety, all covetousness, vainglory and sloth, all malice, all wrath and anger, all remembrance of injuries, every notion of the flesh and spirit that is contrary to thy holy will; and grant us, O Lord, the Lover of men, with freedom, with a pure heart and a contrite soul, without confusion of face, and with sanctified lips, boldly to call upon thee, our Holy God and Father, who art in heaven.

Liturgy of St. Jerome, 2nd Century

13   May the most high Lord bless us all, hallowing us with a perfect spiritual benediction, and make happy our coming in to this holy church . . . Now, O Lord, our God and King, send thy grace upon us, enlighten our hearts and our minds, and enable us wisely to listen to the words of thy holy gospel. And not to hear but also to do, that we may bear good fruit . . . that thou mayest listen to us . . . who pray for the kingdom of Heaven.

The Ethiopic Liturgy

14   O Lord our God, whose power is without limit and whose glory is beyond understanding, whose mercy is vast and whose tenderness is without end, look in thine unutterable love upon thy people and this holy temple and show thy mercy and loving-kindness towards us and all those who in prayer are united with us. For thine is the glory, and the power and the honor, now and for endless ages.

The Liturgy of the Armenians

57

15 O Lord our God, whose power is unspeakable, whose glory is beyond imagining, whose mercy is measureless, whose love for man is above words, look down upon us and this holy house, O Master, and bestow upon all here present the riches of thy goodness and mercy. For to thee belong all glory, honor and worship, Father, Son and Holy Ghost, now and for ever, world without end.

The Byzantine Liturgy

16 Lord God Almighty, thine is the holy universal church. . . . Thou, O Lord, hast by thy loving kindness made us weak men worthy to become appointed members of that great body, the universal church, through which spiritual aids are ministered to the souls of believers. Do thou, therefore, O Lord, fulfil thy grace within us and distribute thy gifts by our hands . . . And grant in thy goodness that we together may be pleasing to thy Godhead all the days of our lives by those good works which are acceptable to thy will, so that we may be worthy, with the help of thy grace, ever to offer thee glory and honor, praise and worship, O Lord of all, Father, Son and Holy Ghost, for ever.

The Liturgy of Malabar, 5th Century

17 O Lord our God, great, eternal, wonderful in glory, who keepest covenant and promise for those that love thee with their whole heart, who art the life of all, the help of those that flee unto thee, the hope of those who cry unto thee, cleanse us from our sins, and from every thought displeasing to thy goodness. Cleanse our souls and bodies, our hearts and consciences, that with a pure heart and a clear mind, with perfect love and calm hope, we may venture confidently and fearlessly to pray unto thee.

Ancient Collects

18 Almighty God, who hast given us grace at this time with one accord to make our common supplication unto thee, and dost promise that when two or three are gathered together in thy Name thou wilt grant their requests; fulfill now, O Lord, the desires and petitions of thy servants, as may be most expedient for them; granting us in this world knowledge of thy truth, and in the world to come life everlasting.

St. John Chrysostom, 345–407

19   Almighty God, who seest that we have no power of ourselves: Keep us, both outwardly in our bodies and inwardly in our souls; that we may be defended from all adversities which may happen to the body, and from all evil thoughts which may assault and hurt the soul.

Gregorian Sacramentary, 8th Century

20   Help us, O Lord, always to wait for thee, to wish for thee, and to watch for thee, that at thy coming again thou mayest find us ready, for thy sake we ask it.

Ancient Collects

21   O God who hast prepared for those who love thee such good things as pass man's understanding; pour into our hearts such love toward thee, that we, loving thee above all things, may obtain thy promises, which exceed all that we can desire.

Gelasian Sacramentary, 6th Century

22   Grant to us, Lord, we beseech thee, the spirit to think and do always such things as are right; that we, who cannot do any thing that is good without thee, may by thee be enabled to live according to thy will; through Jesus Christ our Lord.

Leonine Sacramentary, 5th-6th Century

23   Direct our steps this day, O Lord, unto the way of peace, and strengthen our hearts to obey thy commandments; may the Day-spring visit us from on high, and give light to those who sit in darkness and the shadow of death, that they may adore thee for thy mercy, follow thee for thy truth, desire thee for thy sweetness, who art the blessed Lord God of Israel, both now and evermore.

Ancient Collects

24   Grant us, O Lord, to pass this day in gladness and peace, without stumbling and without stain; that, reaching the eventide victorious over all temptations, we may praise thee, the eternal God, who art blessed, and dost govern all things, world without end. Amen.

Mozarabic Rite, before 8th Century

25   O eternal Light, shine into our hearts. O eternal goodness, deliver us from evil. O eternal Power, be thou our support. Grant unto us that with all our hearts, and minds, and strength, we may ever more seek thy face.

Alcuin, 8th Century

26   Almighty and everlasting God, who art always more ready to hear than we to pray, and art wont to give more than either we desire or deserve; pour down upon us the abundance of thy mercy, forgiving us those things whereof our conscience is afraid, and giving us those good things which we are not worthy to ask, but through the merit and mediation of Jesus Christ, thy Son, our Lord. Amen.

Leonine Sacramentary, 5th-6th Century

27   Our heavenly Father in whom we live and move and have our being, we humbly pray Thee so to guide and govern us by Thy Holy Spirit, that in all the cares and occupations of our daily life we may never forget Thee, but remember that we are ever walking in Thy sight; for Thine own Name's sake.

Ancient Collects

28   O Lord, our heavenly Father, almighty and everlasting God, who hast safely brought us to the beginning of this day; defend us in the same with thy mighty power; and grant that this day we fall into no sin, neither run into any kind of danger; but that all our doings, being ordered by thy governance, may be righteous in thy sight.

Gregorian Sacramentary, 6th Century

29   O Gracious and Holy Father, give us wisdom to perceive thee, intellect to understand thee, diligence to seek thee, patience to wait for thee, eyes to behold thee, a heart to meditate upon thee, and a life to proclaim thee. Amen.

St. Benedict

30   O Lord, we beseech thee mercifully to receive the prayers of thy people who call upon thee; and grant that they may both perceive and know what things they ought to do; and also may have the grace and power faithfully to fulfill the same.

Gregorian Sacramentary, 6th Century

31 O God, who broughtest us from the rest of last night
Unto the joyous light of this day,
Be Thou bringing us from the new light of this day
Unto the guiding light of eternity.

Gaelic

32 We give thee hearty thanks for the rest of the past night, and for the gift of the new day. Grant that we may so pass its hours in the perfect freedom of thy service, that at eventide we may again give thanks unto thee.

The Book of Common Prayer, Canada

33 O God of peace and charity, deliver us from all temptation, assist us in every conflict, console us in every tribulation. Give us patience in adversity, and grace to worship thee with a pure conscience, and to serve Thee with all our strength.

Gelasian Sacramentary, 6th Century

34 Direct us, O Lord, in all our doings, with thy most gracious favor, and further us with thy continual help; that in all our works begun, continued, and ended in thee, we may glorify thy holy Name, and finally, by thy mercy, obtain everlasting life.

Gregorian Sacramentary, 8th Century

35 O God, who through the grace of thy Holy Spirit, dost pour the gift of love into the hearts of thy faithful people; grant unto us health, both of mind and body, that we may love thee with our whole strength, and with entire satisfaction may perform those things which are pleasing unto thee.

Sarum Breviary, 12th Century

36 O God, grant us grace to desire thee with our whole heart; that so desiring we may seek thee and find thee, and so finding thee may love thee.

St. Anselm, 1033–1109

37 Almighty God, unto whom all hearts are open, all desires known, and from whom no secrets are hid, cleanse the thoughts of our hearts by the inspiration of thy Holy Spirit, that we may perfectly love thee, and worthily magnify thy holy Name.

Gregorian Sacramentary, 6th Century

38   Almighty and most merciful God, grant, we beseech thee, that by the indwelling of thy Holy Spirit, we may be enlightened and strengthened for thy service; through Jesus Christ our Lord, who liveth and reigneth with thee in the unity of the same Spirit ever, one God, world without end.

The Book of Common Prayer

39   O Lord our God, who art always more ready to bestow thy good gifts upon us than we are to seek them, and art willing to give more than we desire or deserve; help us to seek that we may truly find, so to ask that we may joyfully receive, so to knock that the door of thy mercy may be opened unto us, through Jesus Christ our Lord. Amen.

The Book of Common Order, Scotland

40   Heavenly Father; this is the hour of prayer, and we come to this place where prayer is wont to be made. We come to thee, who hearest prayer. We thank thee for the prayers thou hast answered; for thou has heard our cry, and hast met our deepest need. We thank thee for the prayers thou hast denied, for often we have asked amiss. Grant us now thy Holy Spirit to help our infirmity, that we may pray as we ought. And before we leave thy house, may the burdens which oppress us fall away, may our strength be renewed, and may we know the peace of those whose sins thou hast forgiven.

A Book of Services and Prayers

41   O Lord, from whom all good things do come; Grant to us thy humble servants that by thy holy inspiration we may think those things that are good, and by thy merciful guiding may perform the same.

The Book of Common Prayer

42   O Thou who are the light of the minds that know thee, the life of the souls that love thee, and the strength of the wills that serve thee, help us to know thee that we may truly love thee, so to love thee that we may fully serve thee, whom to serve is perfect freedom, through Jesus Christ our Lord. Amen.

The Book of Common Order, Scotland

43   Eternal and Holy God, we ask that thou wilt meet with us in this hour of prayer. As we remember thy love to us, may thanksgiving rise from our hearts. As we remember our failures and sins, may we become contrite and humbly beseech thy forgiveness. As we remember the needs of mankind, may we become more sure that Jesus is the Light of the world, the Bread of life, and the Saviour of all men. As we remember our own need, deepen our trust in thee, renew our faith in thy purpose, and grant us some word from thyself for our comfort and help.

A Book of Services and Prayers

44   O Lord, we beseech thee, mercifully to receive the prayers of thy people who call upon thee; and grant that they may both perceive and know what things they ought to do, and also may have grace and power faithfully to fulfil the same.

The Book of Common Prayer

45   Grant, O Lord, that all who worship within this place may present their bodies a living sacrifice, holy, acceptable unto thee; and that they may themselves be temples of the Holy Ghost, wherein thou wilt dwell for evermore.

The Book of Common Prayer, Ireland

46   O God of Peace, who hast taught us that in returning and rest we shall be saved, in quietness and confidence shall be our strength; By the might of thy spirit lift us, we pray thee, to Thy presence where we may be still and know that Thou art God.

The Book of Common Prayer

47   O God, grant that in our worship we may come very near to thee. In all we do, give us grace to follow the leading of thy Holy Spirit. Thou art our shield and shelter; our joy and hope; our strength and life; and our portion evermore. Deepen our faith in thee; enlighten our understanding; sanctify our wills; and let all our thoughts and deeds glorify thee.

A Book of Services and Prayers

48 O Lord, our God, the God of peace and God of love; let thine own peace descend upon us now; and in our weakness and our need uphold us in thy love; that, waiting upon thee in this hour of worship, we may proclaim the wonders of thy grace.

James M. Todd

49 O God, in whom we live and move and have our being,
    by thy Spirit help us to worship thee.
Assured of thy love and mercy,
    may we come humbly to thy throne of grace.
Hungry and thirsty,
    may we find thy Word meat and drink to our souls.
Eager to know and serve thee,
    may we see thy face in Jesus Christ our Lord
    and learn from him the way of life.

R. W. Stewart

50 Almighty and everlasting God, Lord of heaven and earth, of whom, and through whom, and to whom all things are: we glorify thy majesty and grace. Hear us as we call upon thee with the prayer of faith; and so renew our hearts and wills that we may praise thee worthily for thy great love wherewith thou hast redeemed us all.

A Book of Services and Prayers

51 Eternal God, who art always with us, though we often know it not: reveal thyself now, we pray thee, as we seek to enter into the promise of thy most glorious name. Our Father thou art from everlasting: thou has made us, and not we ourselves: and thou hast set us but an handbreadth from thee, that we, thy children, might learn the ways of freedom and choose thee with all our heart. Grant us now thy Holy Spirit, that we may worship thee with gladness, and be confident in prayer, and have the mind of children toward thee.

Book of Common Order, Church of Scotland

52 O God, we would worship thee,
    but without thy help we cannot pray aright.
We have not full assurance of faith,

or else we are easy-minded and overbold.
We are burdened more by worldly cares than by our
   sins.
Come thou to our aid, and guide our thoughts,
Touch our hearts and bend our wills to thine.
Make us, while sure of thy mercy,
   still to wonder at thy grace in Jesus
      Christ our Lord. Amen.

R. W. Stewart

53   Eternal God, who art the Creator of all things and
Father of all men; we bow before thy majesty and thy mercy.
We cannot comprehend thy glory; nor, because of our infirmities, fully trust thy power. But thou art gracious and
full of compassion. Thou hast light for our darkness, faith
for our doubt, peace for our anxiety, rest for our weariness,
and the garment of praise for the spirit of heaviness. They
that seek thee, O Lord, shall not want any manner of thing
that is good. Wherefore of thy fulness let us all rejoice, that
we may worship thee with confidence and joy.

A Book of Services and Prayers

54   Thou, O Lord, art in the midst of us!
   As we have crossed the threshold of this church
May our spirit enter and be at home in the region of
   eternal things.
Let high thoughts come to our minds,
   and pure and fervent desires be awakened.
Let the doubts and fears that grow in darkness
   be overcome and harvested in the light of thy love
   revealed to us in Jesus Christ our Lord. Amen.

R. W. Stewart

55   O Thou with whom is the fountain of life, from whom
cometh every good and perfect gift, whose strength is made
perfect in weakness; be near to us to quicken our faltering
praise, to assist our stammering prayer, and to strengthen
our feeble understanding of thy Word: that those things
which we now do in our worship may set forth thy glory
and magnify thy holy name.

A Book of Services and Prayers

56   O Lord, our God, who art nigh unto all them that call upon thee, to all that call upon thee in truth; make us, we beseech thee, confident in prayer, joyful in praise, and ready to hear and to receive thy Word, that we may know thy peace within our hearts, and glorify the wonders of thy grace.

James M. Todd

57   Heavenly Father, in the midst of our daily toil we pause for these brief moments that we may set our life beneath thy sight. Short is the day of rest; its hours will quickly pass, and the morrow will see us again in the place of our duties and cares. Short is this hour of prayer and praise; help us to worship thee in the beauty of holiness. May we fully know the blessing thou hast for us. Grant us wisdom to understand the life we live, strength to meet its tasks and responsibilities and courage to do the work thou hast entrusted to us. Help us now to see Jesus, in whose face the light of thy glory is revealed. May we know his presence with us. May we become sure of thy forgiveness, sure of thy saving power in our lives. And may we say, as our faith is kindled anew, "We have known and believed the love that God hath for us. God is love."

A Book of Services and Prayers

58   O Lord, open Thou our lips and purify our hearts, that we may worthily magnify Thy holy Name; and help us to be reverent in thought, word, and act, and to worship Thee now and always in the filial faith and spirit of Jesus Christ our Lord.

Devotional Services

59   Almighty God, our heavenly Father, who hast promised to hear us in the name of Jesus Christ thy Son, and who hast taught us in thy Word not to forsake the assembling of ourselves together: we meet in thy presence, dependent on thy promise, and beseech thee to pardon our offences, and so to lift up our thoughts and to draw forth

our desires toward thyself, that seeking thee we may find
thee, and worship thee in spirit and truth.

A Book of Public Worship

60   We praise and magnify thee, O God eternal, for thy
goodness and thy glory. Especially do we thank thee for the
privilege and joy of worship. Thou hast made us to know
thee; thou hast called us to glorify thee; and in thy service
thou hast given our fulfillment and our life. Lift up our
thoughts and all the powers of our mind, so that, in thy
house, proclaiming the wonder of thy grace and mercy in
thy Son our Savior, we may adore thee with rejoicing hearts.

George Phillips

61   Almighty God, our heavenly Father, who reigneth
over all things in thy wisdom, power and love; we humble
ourselves in thy presence, adoring thee for thy glory and
majesty, and praising thee for thy grace and truth revealed
to us in thy Son our Savior. Grant us the help of thy Holy
Spirit, we beseech thee, that we may worship thee in spirit
and in truth.

A Book of Public Worship

62   Almighty God, the Father of our Lord Jesus Christ,
and our Father; help us now as we seek through our prayers
to draw near to thee, bow our wills to thine, and to yield our
spirits to the influence of thy Holy Spirit. Help us as we
would worship thine eternal goodness; meditate on the un-
wearied mercy of which we are constant partakers; confess
our shortcomings and sins, and give ourselves to be led by
thee in ways of purity and peace. In thine infinite love, be
found of our seeking.

Devotional Services

63   O Almighty God, who pourest out on all who desire it,
the spirit of grace and supplication; Deliver us, when we
draw nigh to thee, from coldness of heart and wanderings
of mind, that with steadfast thoughts and kindled affections,
we may worship thee in spirit and in truth.

The Book of Common Prayer

64   Eternal God, who art to be found by those who truly seek thee, if we draw nigh unto thee, thou wilt draw nigh unto us. We pray that we may know thy presence. Hallow our thoughts; uplift our desires; grant us to be reverent before thee. But more than this we ask. The pure in heart shall see thy face; by the forgiving in spirit thy forgiving love is fully known; to those who love thee with all their heart and trust in thy saving grace, the mind of Christ is given. Wherefore, in thy mercy, deliver us from every impurity and selfishness; from everything that prevents our discerning and doing thy holy will. And grant that, thus forgiving and forgiven and cleansed from our sins, we may worship thee in spirit and in truth.

A Book of Services and Prayers

65   Most holy and most Gracious God, who turnest the shadow of night into morning, satisfy us early with thy mercy, that we may rejoice and be glad all the day. Lift the light of thy countenance upon us; calm every troubled thought; and guide our feet into the way of peace. Perfect thy strength in our weakness, and help us to worship thee.

Devotional Services

66   O Lord, our heavenly Father, at the beginning of another week we come to thee for help and light. Grant, we beseech thee, that we may hallow this day of rest to thy service, and find in thee all peace and strength. Quicken our devotion that we may serve thee in spirit and in truth, and lay a good foundation for our coming week. Be with us in all the public services of thy day, that we may join in them with heart and soul, and receive the blessing which thou hast promised to all who sincerely pray to thee and faithfully hear thy word. This we ask for the sake of Jesus Christ our Lord.

Bishop Brooke Foss Westcott, 1825–1901

67   O God, who givest us these quiet moments of holy thought and prayer, mercifully receive our worship, and grant that we may continually advance in the love of Thee, and be able evermore to abide in Thy peace.

Devotional Services

68   O Thou eternal God, speak to each of us the word that we need, and let thy word abide with us until it has wrought

in us thy holy will. Cleanse, quicken, and refresh our hearts; direct and increase our faith; and grant that we, by our worship at this time, may be enabled to see thee more clearly, to love thee more fully, and to serve thee more perfectly.

Devotional Services

69   Almighty and everlasting God, in whom we live and move and have our being, who hast created us for thyself, so that our hearts are restless till they find rest in thee, grant unto us purity of heart and strength of purpose so that no selfish passion may hinder us from knowing thy will, and no weakness from doing it. In thy light may we see life clearly, and in thy service find perfect freedom. For thy mercy's sake.

Prayers and Services

70   O God, whose Spirit searchest all things, and whose love bearest all things, encourage us to draw near to thee in sincerity and in truth. Save us from a worship of the lips while our hearts are far away. Save us from the useless labour of attempting to conceal ourselves from thee who searchest the heart.

Make us strong enough to bear the vision of the truth, and to have done with all falsehood, pretence, and hypocrisy, so that we may see things as they are, and fear no more . . . And may we have the grace of gratitude, and the desire to dedicate ourselves to Thee.

William E. Orchard

71   O Lord God, heavenly Father; we beseech thee, let thy Holy Spirit dwell in us, that he may enlighten and lead us into all truth, and evermore defend us from all adversities, through Jesus Christ thy Son, our God.

Common Service Book

72   O Thou who makest the stars and turnest the shadow of death into the morning: We render thee, our Lord and King, the tribute of our praise for this new day, for the ever lasting hopes that rise within the human heart, and for the gospel which has brought life and immortality to light.

The Kingdom, the Power, and the Glory

73   Grant us, O our God and Father, the strength and courage to fulfill the noble resolve of our hearts. May our faith in Thee, nurtured in this house and kept ablaze by our prayers, ever shine before us, so that amid the hardships and distractions of daily life we may retain a vision of Thy greatness and glory.

Union Prayer Book

74   Eternal, Holy, Almighty, whose name is Love, we are met in solemn company to seek thy face, and in spirit and truth to worship thy name. We come in deep humility, since thou art high and exalted, and because thou beholdest the proud afar off . . . We come in the name and spirit of Jesus to make our wills one with thine.

William E. Orchard

75   God of Compassion, if anyone has come to thine altar troubled in spirit, depressed and apprehensive, expecting to go away as he came, with the same haunting heaviness of heart; if anyone is deeply wounded of soul, hardly daring to hope that anything can afford him the relief he seeks, so surprised by the ill that life can do that he is half afraid to pray: O God surprise him, we beseech thee, by the graciousness of thy help; and enable him to take from thy bounty as ungrudgingly as thou givest, that he may leave here his sorrow and take a song away; we ask in the name of Jesus.

Common Service Book

76   O Lord, who hast brought us through the darkness of night to the light of morning, and who, by thy Holy Spirit, dost illumine the darkness of ignorance and sin: We beseech thee of thy loving-kindness to pour thy holy light into our souls, that we may be ever devoted to thee, by whose wisdom we were created, by whose mercy we were redeemed, and by whose providence we are governed, to the honor and glory of thy great name.

The Kingdom, the Power, and the Glory

77   Almighty God, the fountain of all wisdom, who knowest our necessities before we ask, and our ignorance in ask-

ing; we beseech thee to have compassion upon our infirmities; and those things which for our unworthiness we dare not, and for our blindness we cannot ask, vouchsafe to give us, for the worthiness of Jesus Christ Thy Son, our Lord.

Common Service Book

78   Thou, who art the source of all blessings, be with this congregation and all its members, their families and their households; prosper them in their various callings and occupations, help them in their needs, and guide them in their difficulties. Hear thou the prayers of all who worship here this morning, comfort the sorrowing and cheer the silent sufferers. Bless those who guide and who serve this congregation and those who contribute to its strength. Reward with the joy of goodness the charitable and the merciful who aid the poor, care for the sick, teach the ignorant, and extend a helping hand to those who have lost their way in the world.

Union Prayer Book

79   O God our Father, may the meditations of our hearts in this hour, be acceptable in thy sight; may we strive for a new understanding of thy word and will; may we here resolve upon a more complete obedience to thy commands, a richer ministry to thy people and purpose. Through thy Spirit lift us up into a greater steadfastness, a finer courage, a fuller loyalty, and a devotion worthy of those who name themselves after thee; through Jesus Christ our Lord.

Lisgar R. Eckardt

80   God and Father, we have entered Thy sanctuary on this Sabbath to hallow Thy name and to offer unto thee prayers of thanksgiving. The week of toil is ended, the day of rest has come. Thou, Creator of all, hast given us the blessing of labor, so that by our work we may fashion things of use and beauty. May the fruit of our work be acceptable unto Thee. May each new Sabbath find us going from strength to strength, so that by Thy grace we may be helped to even worthier work.

Union Prayer Book

81   O Thou, in whose life we find our life, through the gift of whose spirit we do our work and bear our burdens; grant us now the sense of thy nearness. We would open our hearts freely to thy Spirit, our minds to thy law, and our wills to thy quickening energy. Dwell in us and make us fruitful.

82   O God, thou source of all pure desires and holy affections, give us now a quiet mind and a reverent heart, that we may worthily worship thee at this time.

The Pilgrim Hymnal

83   Our God and God of our Fathers, grant that our worship on this Sabbath be acceptable to Thee. May we, sanctified through thy commandments, become sharers in the blessing of thy word. Teach us to be satisfied with the gifts of thy goodness and gratefully to rejoice in all thy mercies. Purify our hearts that we may serve thee in truth. O help us to preserve the Sabbath . . . that it may ever bring rest and joy, peace and comfort to the dwellings of our brethren, and through it thy name be hallowed in all the earth.

Union Prayer Book

84   Fix our steps, O Lord, that we stagger not at the uneven motions of the world, but go steadily on our way, neither censuring our journey by the weather we meet, nor turning aside for anything that befalls us.

John Austin, 18th Century

85   We gratefully acknowledge, O Lord our God, that Thou art our Creator and Preserver, the rock of our life and the shield of our help. We render thanks unto Thee for our lives which are in thy hand, for our souls which are ever in thy keeping, for thy wondrous providence and for thy continued goodness, which Thou bestowest upon us day by day. Truly, thy mercies never fail and thy loving-kindness never ceases. Therefore do we forever put our trust in Thee.

Union Prayer Book

86   O God, from whom all holy desires, all good counsels, and all just works do proceed: Give unto Thy servants that peace which the world cannot give; that our hearts may be

set to obey Thy commandments, and also that by Thee we, being defended from the fear of our enemies, may pass our time in rest and quietness.

The Book of Common Prayer

87   O Thou who didst come into the world to be its light, and Who still art daily teaching us in all the experiences of life: as the malice of Thine enemies was frustrated by the eager attention of those who were determined to hear Thy word, grant unto us, we beseech Thee, a like determination, that by our faithful waiting upon Thee in Thy temple we may defeat the malice and thwart the evil designs of those powers that would destroy Thy gracious influence in the world.

Let Us Worship God

88   Almighty and everlasting God, whom the heaven of heavens cannot contain, much less the temples which our hands have builded, but who art ever nigh unto the humble and the contrite; shed down the Holy Spirit, we beseech Thee, on all who are here assembled: that cleansed and illumined by thy grace, we may worthily show forth thy praise, meekly learn thy word, render due thanks for thy mercies, and obtain a gracious answer to our prayers, through Jesus Christ our Lord.

A Manual of Meditation

89   O Eternal God, by whom the whole Body of Christ is sustained and governed, we thank Thee that Thou hast called us to worship Thee in Thy holy church. Grant to us each day to feel more deeply the privileges of Christian fellowship. Bless to us all the services of public worship, and in our present waiting upon Thee in this Thy house. Reveal Thyself to us, according to thy promises, in the appointed means of grace. Give a rich increase to each seed of good sown in our hearts; and by Thy almighty power keep us steadfast in the faith once delivered to the saints, through Jesus Christ our Lord.

Let Us Worship God

90   O Lord, our heavenly Father, who orderest all things for our eternal good, mercifully enlighten our minds, give us a firm and abiding trust in Thy love and care. Silence our murmurings, quiet our fears, and dispel our doubts, that, rising above our afflictions and anxieties, we may rest on Thee, the Rock of everlasting Strength.

New Church Book of Worship, 1876

91   O God, who makest thyself known in the stillness; let us feel thy presence in this sacred place; make us to be of the company of brave saints who have worshipped here in spirit and in truth; through the voices of men and the instruments of praise give us to lift our heart to thee; and so, O Lord, purify our lives that going forth into the world, we may go in thy strength and in thy love, through Jesus Christ our Lord.

Charles Lewis Slattery, 1867–1930

92   Most gracious God, who art ever more ready to hear than we are to pray; who knowest our necessities before we ask and our ignorance in asking, behold us here, coming from all our various homes and works, with all our different faults and needs, asking in a common prayer for light upon our way and for peace within our hearts.

Francis G. Peabody, 1847–1941

93   O God, who puttest into our hearts such deep desires that we cannot be at peace until we rest in thee: mercifully grant that the longing of our souls may not go unsatisfied because of any unrighteousness of life that may separate us from thee. Open our minds to the counsels of eternal wisdom; breathe into our souls the peace which passeth understanding. Increase our hunger and thirst for righteousness, and feed us, we beseech thee, with the bread of heaven. Give us grace to seek first thy kingdom, and help us to know that thou wilt add unto us all things needful.

94   Almighty God, who art our Father, we lift up our hearts to thee, invoking thy blessing and benediction upon our worship. Thou hast made us one in our need of thee, one in our desire for thy fellowship, one in common hope of life

everlasting; and we beseech thee now to unite us in the holy communion of prayer. Cleanse our hearts and our hands, that we may ascend to thy holy hill, and worship the Lord in the beauty of holiness. We give thee thanks, O Lord, for this day of prayer, and for this place of quiet, set amid our hurrying life, hallowed by the memories of days gone by, and dedicated to the life of the soul and the service of faith. May it be to us a place of rest and joy, of light and revelation; so manifest thyself to us that all that is best in us may be called forth to praise thee, who art the health of our countenance and our God. (abridged)

Joseph Fort Newton, 1878–1950

95   O God, . . . visit, we pray thee, this congregation and each of us with thy indwelling spirit; unite us in fellowship with thy worshippers in all lands; and grant that our thoughts and words and the unspoken longings of our hearts may be acceptable in thy sight, and may be offered in the name of our Master, Jesus Christ.

Elmore McNeil McKee

96   Almighty God, our Heavenly Father, Who hast made the Church Thy dwelling place, and hast taught us in Thy word not to forsake the assembling of ourselves together: regard us in Thy mercy, we beseech thee, who meet this day in this Thy holy place; manifest Thyself unto us, and bless us that our worship may prepare us both to serve Thee now and to glorify Thee in Thine eternal Kingdom.

97   We commend unto Thee, O Lord,
    our souls and our bodies,
    our minds and our thoughts,
    our prayers and our hopes,
    our health and our work,
    our life and our death;
    our parents and brothers and sister,
    our benefactors and friends,
    our neighbors, our countrymen,
    and all Christian folk
    this day and always. Amen.

Lancelot Andrewes, 1555–1626

98 O Lord God of our Life, who hast given us the rest of this sacred day, grant that the benediction of its restfulness may abide upon us throughout the week. Enable us to carry the influence of its consecration unto all that we do; let the praises of our lips rendered to thee this day become praise in our lives. May the power of thy love be with us in every duty; that by pureness, by knowledge, and by courage we may glorify thee.

99 Almighty God, by whom alone kings reign and princes decree justice; and from whom alone cometh all counsel, wisdom, and understanding; we thine unworthy servants, here gathered together in thy Name, we most humbly beseech thee to send down thy heavenly wisdom from above, to direct and guide us in all our consultations: and grant that, we having thy fear always before our eyes, and laying aside all private interests, prejudices, and partial affections, the result of all our counsels may be the glory of thy blessed Name, the maintenance of true religion and justice, the safety, honour, and happiness of . . . the public welfare, peace and tranquility of the realm, and the uniting and knitting together of the hearts of all persons and estates within the same, in true Christian charity and love one towards another, through Jesus Christ our Lord and Savior.

17th-Century prayer used in Parliament

100   Let thy blessing rest upon this church, O Lord,
      Out from the by-roads, out of our care-filled days
      We come, an earnest throng to hear Thy word.
      To offer Thee our sincere, heartfelt praise,
      We come to seek thy steadfast guiding power,
      We come to lay our burdens at Thy feet;
      We seek the calming quiet of this hour
      Away from the clamoring throng, the crowded street.

      Let thy blessing rest upon this church, we pray,
      Upon a people in their vital need;
      Be thou our helper, be our guide and stay,
      And be our wine, the bread on which we feed.
      Lord God, for every church in every land,
      We crave a blessing from Thy mighty hand.

101   Teach us, good Lord,
      to serve thee as thou deservest:

to give and not to count the cost;
to fight and not to heed the wounds;
to strive and not to seek for rest;
to labor and not to ask for reward,
Save in the knowledge that we do thy will.

St. Ignatius Loyola, 1491–1556

102   We give thee hearty thanks, O Lord, for rest during the past night, and for the gift of a new day with its many opportunities of pleasing thee. Grant that we may so pass its hours in the perfect freedom of thy praise, that at eventide we may again give thanks unto thee; through Jesus Christ our Lord.

Eastern Orthodox Church Daybreak Service

103   Bless, O Lord, all who worship thee, from the rising of the sun unto the going down of the same. Of thy goodness give us, with thy love inspire us, by thy spirit guide us, in thy power protect us, in thy mercy receive us, now and always.

Devotional Services

104   Watch Thou, dear Lord, with those who wake, or watch, or weep tonight, and give Thine angels charge over those who sleep. Tend thy sick ones, O Lord Christ. Rest Thy weary ones. Bless Thy dying ones. Soothe Thy suffering ones. Pity Thine afflicted ones. Shield Thy joyous ones. And all, for Thy Love's sake.

St. Augustine, 354–430

105   Lord of the evening hour, who hast often met with us at the close of day, be our Refuge now from the noise of the world and the care of our own spirits. Grant us Thy peace. Let not the darkness of our ignorance and fallow, of our sorrow and sin hide Thee from us. Draw near to us that we may be near to Thee. Speak to each of us the word that we need, and let thy word abide in us till it has wrought in us thy holy will. Quicken and refresh our hearts, renew and increase our strength, so that we may grow into the likeness of thy faithful children, and by our worship at this time be enabled better to serve thee in our daily life in the spirit of Jesus Christ our Lord.

Devotional Services

106 O Thou who alone makest us to dwell in safety: refresh with quiet sleep this night those who are wearied with the labors of the day; and mercifully protect from harm all who put their trust in thee, that, lying down in peace to take our rest, we may fear no evil, but confidently give ourselves into thy holy keeping as becometh disciples of Jesus Christ, in whom we see and realize Thy great love.

Devotional Services

107 Be present, O merciful God, and protect us through the silent hours of this night, so that we who are wearied by the changes and chances of this fleeting world may repose upon thine unchanging love.

The Kingdom, the Power, and the Glory

IV

Sentences
Before
Scripture

1   These words which I command you this day shall be upon your heart; and you shall teach them diligently to your children, and shall talk of them when you sit in your house, and when you walk by the way, and when you lie down, and when you rise.

Deuteronomy 6:6–7

2   The law of the Lord is perfect, reviving the soul
the testimony of the Lord is sure, making wise the
    simple;
the precepts of the Lord are right, rejoicing the heart;
the commandment of the Lord is pure, enlightening
    the eyes;
the fear of the Lord is clean, enduring for ever;
the ordinances of the Lord are true, and righteous
    altogether.

Psalms 19:7–9

3   How can a young man keep his way pure?
    By guarding it according to thy word.

Psalms 119:9

4   I have laid up thy word in my heart,
    that I might not sin against thee.
Blessed be thou, O Lord;
    teach me thy statutes!

Psalms 119:11–12

5   Thy word is a lamp to my feet
    and a light to my path.

Psalms 119:105

6   The unfolding of thy words gives light;
    it imparts understanding to the simple.

Psalms 119:130

7   Blessed rather are those who hear the word of God and keep it!

Luke 11:28

8   In the beginning was the Word, and the Word was with God, and the Word was God. And the Word became

flesh and dwelt among us, full of grace and truth; we have beheld his glory, glory as of the only Son from the Father.

John 1:1, 14

9   These are written that you may believe that Jesus is the Christ, the Son of God, and that believing you may have life in his name.

John 20:31

10   Whatever was written in former days was written for our instruction, that by steadfastness and by the encouragement of the scriptures we might have hope.

Romans 15:4

11   Let the word of Christ dwell in you rightly, as you teach and admonish one another in all wisdom, and as you sing psalms and hymns and spiritual songs with thankfulness in your hearts to God.

Colossians 3:16

12   All scripture is inspired by God and profitable for teaching, for reproof, for correction, and for training in righteousness that the man of God may be complete, equipped for every good work.

II Timothy 3:16–17

13   For the word of God is living and active, sharper than any two-edged sword, piercing to the division of soul and spirit, of joints and marrow, and discerning the thoughts and intentions of the heart.

Hebrews 4:12

14   But be ye doers of the word, and not hearers only, deceiving yourselves.

James 1:22

15   All flesh is like grass and all its glory like the flower of grass. The grass withers, and the flower fails, but the word of the Lord abides for ever. That word is the good news which was preached to you.

I Peter 1:24–25

V

Sentences
and
Prayers After
Scripture

A. FROM THE OLD TESTAMENT

1 Make me to know thy ways, O Lord;
    teach me thy paths.
  Lead me in thy truth, and teach me,
    for thou art the God of my salvation.

Psalms 25:4–5

2 There is none like thee among the gods, O Lord,
    nor are there any works like thine.

Psalms 86:8

3 Teach me thy way, O Lord,
    that I may walk in thy truth;
    unite my heart to fear thy name.

Psalms 86:11

4 I give thanks to thee, O Lord my God, with my
    whole heart,
  and I will glorify thy name for ever.

Psalms 86:12

5 Bless the Lord, O my soul;
    and all that is within me, bless his holy name!

Psalms 103:1

6 Praise the Lord, all nations!
    Extol him, all peoples!
  For great is his steadfast love toward us;
    and the faithfulness of the Lord endures for ever.
  Praise the Lord!

Psalms 117:1–2

7 Blessed are those whose way is blameless,
    who walk in the law of the Lord!
  Blessed are those who keep his testimonies,
    who seek him with their whole heart.

Psalms 119:1–2

8 How can a young man keep his way pure?
    By guarding it according to thy word.

With my whole heart I seek thee;
    let me not wander from thy commandments.

Psalms 119:9–10

9   Blessed be thou, O Lord;
        teach me thy statutes!
    With my lips I declare
        all the ordinances of thy mouth.
    In the way of thy testimonies I delight
        as much as in all riches.
    I will meditate on thy precepts,
        and fix my eyes on thy ways.
    I will delight in thy statutes;
        I will not forget thy word.

Psalms 119:12–16

10   I will keep thy law continually,
        for ever and ever;
    and I shall walk at liberty,
        for I have sought thy precepts.
    I will also speak of thy testimonies before kings,
        and shall not be put to shame;
    for I find my delight in thy commandments,
        which I love.
    I revere thy commandments, which I love,
        and I will meditate on thy statutes.

Psalms 119:44–48

11   In thy steadfast love spare my life,
        that I may keep the testimonies of thy mouth.

Psalms 119:88

12   Thy testimonies are wonderful;
        therefore my soul keeps them.
    The unfolding of thy words gives light;
        it imparts understanding to the simple.

Psalms 119:129–130

13   Thy righteousness is righteous for ever,
        and thy law is true.

Psalms 119:142

14 Thy testimonies are righteous for ever;
        give me understanding that I may live.
    With my whole heart I cry; answer me, O Lord!
        I will keep thy statutes.

                                    Psalms 119:144–145

15 The sum of thy word is truth;
        and every one of thy righteous ordinances
        endures for ever.

                                    Psalms 119:160

16 Teach me to do thy will,
        for thou art my God!
    Let thy good spirit lead me
        on a level path!

                                    Psalms 143:10

17 The grass withers, the flower fades;
        but the word of our God will stand for ever.

                                    Isaiah 40:8

B. FROM THE NEW TESTAMENT

18 God so loved the world that he gave his only Son, that whoever believes in him should not perish but have eternal life.

                                    John 3:16

19 If you continue in my word, you are truly my disciples, and you will know the truth, and the truth will make you free.

                                    John 8:31–32

20 Thy word is truth.

                                    John 17:17

21 These are written that you may believe that Jesus is the Christ, the Son of God, and that believing you may have life in his name.

                                    John 20:31

22   For the word of the cross is folly to those who are perishing, but to us who are being saved it is the power of God.

I Corinthians 1:18

23   All this is from God, who through Christ reconciled us to himself and gave us the ministry of reconciliation; that is, God was in Christ reconciling the world to himself.

II Corinthians 5:18–19

24   Now to him who by the power at work within us is able to do far more abundantly than all that we ask or think, to him be glory in the church and in Christ Jesus to all generations, for ever and ever. Amen.

Ephesians 3:20–21

25   Set your minds on things that are above, not on things that are on earth.

Colossians 3:2

26   The saying is sure and worthy of full acceptance, that Christ Jesus came into the world to save sinners.

I Timothy 1:15

27   Since we are surrounded by so great a cloud of witnesses, let us also lay aside every weight, and sin which clings so closely, and let us run with perseverance the race that is set before us, looking to Jesus the pioneer and perfecter of our faith.

Hebrews 12:1–2

28   Jesus Christ is the same yesterday and today and forever.

Hebrews 13:8

29   And we have the prophetic word made more sure. You will do well to pay attention to this as to a lamp shining in a dark place, until the day dawns and the morning star rises in your hearts.

II Peter 1:19

30   If we walk in the light, as he is in the light, we have fellowship with one another.

I John 1:7

31   And the world passes away, and the lust of it; but he who does the will of God abides for ever.

I John 2:17

32   See what love the Father has given us, that we should be called children of God; and so we are.

I John 3:1

33   Beloved, if God so loved us, we also ought to love one another.

I John 4:11

34   Every one who believes that Jesus is the Christ is a child of God.

I John 5:1

35   This is the love of God, that we keep his commandments. And his commandments are not burdensome.

I John 5:3

36   Now to him who is able to keep you from falling and to present you without blemish before the presence of his glory with rejoicing, to the only God, our Savior, through Jesus Christ our Lord be glory, majesty, dominion, and authority, before all time and now and for ever. Amen.

Jude 1:24–25

37   He who has an ear, let him hear what the Spirit says to the churches.

Revelation 2:11

38   Worthy art thou, our Lord and God, to receive glory and honor and power, for thou didst create all things, and by thy will they existed and were created.

Revelation 4:11

C.   FROM OTHER SOURCES

39   Thou dost favorably grant knowledge unto men,
And dost teach discernment unto men;
Grant us from Thee knowledge and understanding
and discernment.

Blessed art Thou who dost graciously grant knowledge.

Ancient Hebrew Benediction

40 Here endeth the reading from the Scriptures.

41 May God's name be praised.

42 Here endeth the reading of God's Holy Word as recorded in the _____ chapter of the book of _____.

43. May God add a blessing to us as we ponder the meaning of this His Word.

44 Blessed Lord, by whose providence all Holy Scriptures were written and preserved for our instruction, give us grace to study them this and every day, with patience and love. Strengthen our souls with the fullness of their divine teaching. Keep from us all pride and irreverence. Guide us in the deep things of thy heavenly wisdom, and of thy great mercy lead us by thy Word unto everlasting life; through Jesus Christ our Lord and Saviour. Amen.

Book of Common Worship

45 Blessed Lord, who hast caused all Holy Scriptures to be written for our learning; grant that we may in such wise hear them, read, mark, learn and inwardly digest them, that by patience and comfort of thy holy Word, we may embrace, and ever hold fast, the blessed hope of everlasting life, which thou hast given us in our Saviour Jesus Christ. Amen.

Book of Common Prayer

46 Write upon our hearts, O Lord God, the lessons of thy holy Word, and grant that we may all be doers of the same, and not forgetful hearers only, through Jesus Christ our Lord. Amen.

A. C. Fraser

47 O God, whose Word is quick and powerful, and sharper than any two edged sword, grant us grace to receive thy truth in faith and love, that by it we may be taught and guided, upheld and comforted, and prepared unto every good word and work, to the glory of thy name, through Jesus Christ our Lord. Amen.

Book of Public Worship

48   May God bless to us the reading of His Holy Word, and to His name be glory and praise.

49   O Lord, thy Word is before us, give us a meek, reverent, and teachable mind, whilst we read and study it. Open to us its sacred truths, and enable us to receive it, not as the word of men, but as the Word of God, which liveth and abideth forever. Be thou, O Blessed Spirit, our teacher, enlighten our minds and prepare our hearts. Shine, O Lord, upon thine own sacred page, and make it clear to us. What we see not, show us, and where we are wrong, correct us. Bring home some portion to our souls and thus make us wise unto salvation; through Jesus Christ our Saviour. Amen.

Book of Common Worship

50   Unto the Triune God be adoration, praise and glory, throughout all ages, world without end.

51   Unveil our eyes that we may behold wonderful things out of thy law.

52   O Lord God who has left unto us thy holy word to be a lamp unto our feet and a light unto our path, give unto us all thy holy spirit, we humbly pray thee, that out of the same Word we may learn what is thy blessed will, and frame our lives in all holy obedience to the same, to thine honor and glory and the increase of our faith, through Jesus Christ our Lord. Amen

Book of Common Worship

53   Praised be Thou, O Lord, our God, Ruler of the world, who hast given us the law of truth and hast implanted within us everlasting life. Praised be Thou O Lord, giver of the Law.

Union Prayer Book

54   Almighty, our gracious Father, forasmuch as all our salvation depends upon our having truly understood thy holy Word: therefore grant us that our hearts be set free from worldly things, so that we may with all diligence and faith hear and apprehend thy holy Word, that thereby we may rightly understand thy gracious will, and in all sin-

cerity live according to the same, to thy praise and glory, through Jesus Christ our Lord. Amen.

William D. Maxwell

55 Eternal God, we thank Thee that Thou has granted unto us to hear Thy Word and to proclaim it; to call upon Thee and to praise Thee; and to serve Thee in Thy holy offices. Amen.

Adalbert R. Kretzmann

56 Almighty God, by whose grace we hear the word of thy kingdom, and who hast taught us that they that hear the Word of God and keep it are blessed; grant us so to hear it and to understand it that it may be the rule of our faith and lives, and that we may love it and meditate in it day and night: through Jesus Christ our Lord. Amen.

A Book of Public Worship

57 O Lord, let not thy Word become a judgment upon us, that we hear it and do it not, that we know it and love it not, that we believe it and obey it not.

58 O God, grant that thy Word may be a lamp unto our feet, and a light upon our path. Give us wisdom to discern its teaching and patience to apply it, with such sincerity of heart that our deeds may conform to its instruction.

59 Grant, O God, that whensoever our eyes are holden that we see thee not, our hearts may be attentive to thy Holy Word, and burn within us as it is opened to us by thy Son, our Saviour Jesus Christ.

The Book Annexed, 1883

60 Grant, O Lord, that by thy Holy Word which shall be read and preached in this place, and by thy Holy Spirit grafting it inwardly in the heart, the hearers thereof may both perceive and know what things they ought to do, and may have power and strength to fulfil the same. Amen.

The Book of Common Prayer

VI

Invitations
and
Exhortations to Prayer

A. FROM THE OLD TESTAMENT

1 The eternal God is your dwelling place, and underneath are the everlasting arms.

Deuteronomy 33:27

2 For the Lord sees not as man sees; man looks on the outward appearance, but the Lord looks on the heart.

I Samuel 16:7

3 Thine, O Lord, is the greatness, and the power and the glory, and the victory, and the majesty; for all that is in the heavens and in the earth is thine; thine is the kingdom, O Lord, and thou art exalted as head above all.

I Chronicles 29:11

4 Both riches and honor come from thee, and thou rulest over all. In thy hand are power and might; and in thy hand it is to make great and to give strength to all. And now we thank thee, our God, and praise thy glorious name.

I Chronicles 29:12–13

5 If my people who are called by my name humble themselves and pray and seek my face, and turn from their wicked ways, then I will hear from heaven, and will forgive their sin and heal their land. Now my eyes will be open and my ears attentive to the prayer that is made in this place. For now I have chosen and consecrated this house that my name may be there for ever; my eyes and my heart will be there for all time.

II Chronicles 7:14–16

6 The Lord your God is gracious and merciful, and will not turn away his face from you, if you return to him.

II Chronicles 30:9

7 The good Lord pardon everyone who sets his heart to seek God, the Lord, the God of his fathers.

II Chronicles 30:18–19

8 O Lord, let thy ear be attentive to the prayer of thy servant, and to the prayer of thy servants who delight to

fear thy name; and give success to thy servant today, and grant him mercy in the sight of this man.

Nehemiah 1:11

9   If the Almighty is your gold, and your precious silver;
     Then you will delight yourself in the Almighty
          and lift up your face to God.
     You will make your prayer to him, and he will hear
          you; and you will pay your vows. . . . and light
          will shine on your ways.

Job 22:25–28

10   Give ear to my words, O Lord;
          give heed to my groaning.
     Hearken to the sound of my cry,
          My King and my God,
          for to thee do I pray.

Psalms 5:1–2

11   I will give thanks to the Lord with my whole heart;
     I will tell of all thy wonderful deeds.
     I will be glad and exult in thee,
     I will sing praise to thy name, O Most High.

Psalms 9:1–2

12   O Lord, who shall sojourn in thy tent?
     Who shall dwell on thy holy hill?
     He who walks blamelessly, and does what is right,
          and speaks truth from his heart;
          He who does these things shall never be moved.

Psalms 1:2, 5

13   I love thee, O Lord, my strength. The Lord is my rock, and my fortress, and my deliverer, my God, my rock, in whom I take refuge, my shield, and the horn of my salvation, my stronghold. I call upon the Lord, who is worthy to be praised.

Psalms 18:1–3

14   Let the words of my mouth and the meditations of my heart be acceptable in thy sight, O Lord, my rock and my redeemer.

Psalms 19:14

15   Who shall ascend the hill of the Lord?
And who shall stand in his holy place?
He who has clean hands and a pure heart,
   who does not lift up his soul to what is false,
   and does not swear deceitfully.

Psalms 24:3–4

16   Make me to know thy ways, O Lord;
   teach me thy paths.
Lead me in thy truth, and teach me,
   for thou art the God of my salvation;
   for thee I wait all the day long.

Psalms 25:4–5

17   Remember not the sins of my youth, or my transgressions; according to thy steadfast love remember me,
for thy goodness' sake, O Lord!

Psalms 25:7

18   The friendship of the Lord is for those who fear him,
and he makes known to them his covenant.

Psalms 25:14

19   Turn thou to me, and be gracious to me;
   for I am lonely and afflicted.
Relieve the troubles of my heart,
   and bring me out of my distresses.
Consider my affliction and my trouble,
   and forgive all my sins.

Psalms 25:16–18

20   The Lord is my light and my salvation;
   whom shall I fear?
The Lord is the stronghold of my life;
   of whom shall I be afraid?
For he will hide me in his shelter
   in the day of trouble;
He will conceal me under the cover of his tent,
   he will set me high upon a rock.

Psalms 27:1, 5

21   Wait for the Lord;
        be strong, and let your heart take courage;
     Yea, wait for the Lord!

                                             Psalms 27:14

22   Be strong, and let your heart take courage,
        all you who wait for the Lord.

                                             Psalms 31:24

23   Trust in the Lord, and do good;
     Take delight in the Lord,
        and he will act.
     Be still before the Lord, and wait
        patiently for him.

                                          Psalms 37:3–5, 7

24   I waited patiently for the Lord;
        he inclined to me and heard my cry.

                                             Psalms 40:1

25   As a hart longs for flowing streams,
        so longs my soul for thee, O God.
     My soul thirsts for God,
        for the living God.
     When shall I come and behold
        the face of God?

                                            Psalms 42:1–2

26   Why are you cast down, O my soul,
        and why are you disquieted within me?
     Hope in God; for I shall again praise him,
        my help and my God.

                                             Psalms 43:5

27   O Lord, open thou my lips,
        and my mouth shall show forth thy praise.
     For thou hast no delight in sacrifice;
        were I to give a burnt offering, thou wouldst
        not be pleased.

                                          Psalms 51:15–17

28   Give ear to my prayer, O God;
        and hide not thyself from my supplication
     Attend to me, and answer me.

                                            Psalms 55:1–2

29   I call upon God;
      and the Lord will save me.
    Evening and morning and at noon
      I utter my complaint and moan,
      and he will hear my voice.

Psalms 55:16–17

30   Cast your burden on the Lord
      and he will sustain you;
    he will never permit
      the righteous to be moved.

Psalms 55:22

31   Trust in him at all times, O people;
      pour out your heart before him;
      God is a refuge for us.

Psalms 62:8

32   Blessed be God,
      because he has not rejected my prayer
      or removed his steadfast love from me!

Psalms 66:20

33   May all who seek thee
      rejoice and be glad in thee!
    May those who love thy salvation
      say evermore, "God is great!"

Psalms 70:4

34   We give thanks to thee, O God;
      we give thanks;
    we call on thy name and recount
      thy wondrous deeds.

Psalms 75:1

35   Thou art my God; be gracious to me, O Lord,
      for to thee do I cry all the day.
    Gladden the soul of thy servant,
      for to thee, O Lord, do I lift up my soul.
    For thou, O Lord, art good and forgiving,
      abounding in steadfast love to all who call on thee.
    Give ear, O Lord, to my prayer;
      hearken to my cry of supplication.

In the day of my trouble I call on thee,
for thou dost answer me.

Psalms 86:3–7

36 It is good to give thanks to the Lord,
to sing praises to thy name, O Most High;
To declare thy steadfast love in the morning,
and thy faithfulness by night.

Psalms 92:1–2

37 O come, let us worship and bow down,
let us kneel before the Lord, our Maker!
For he is our God,
and we are the people of his pasture,
and the sheep of his hand.

Psalms 95:6–7

38 Bless the Lord, O my soul;
and all that is within me, bless his holy name!
Bless the Lord, O my soul,
and forget not all his benefits,
who forgives all your iniquity,
who heals all your diseases,
who redeems your life from the Pit,
who crowns you with steadfast love and mercy,
who satisfies you with good as long as you live
so that your youth is renewed like the eagle's.

Psalms 103:1–5

39 I will sing to the Lord as long as I live;
I will sing praise to my God while I have being.
May my meditation be pleasing to him,
for I rejoice in the Lord.

Psalms 104:33–34

40 Remember the wonderful works that he has done,
his miracles, and the judgments he uttered.

Psalms 105:5

41 The fear of the Lord is the beginning of wisdom;
a good understanding have all those who practice it.
His praise endures for ever!

Psalms 111:10

42 Out of my distress I called on the Lord;
      the Lord answered me and set me free.

Psalms 118:5

43 It is better to take refuge in the Lord than to put
      confidence in man.

Psalms 118:8

44 I lift up my eyes to the hills.
      From whence does my help come?
    My help comes from the Lord,
      who made heaven and earth.

Psalms 121:1–2

45 The Lord is your keeper;
      the Lord is your shade
      on your right hand.
    The sun shall not smite you by day,
      nor the moon by night.
    The Lord will keep you from all evil;
      he will keep your life.
    The Lord will keep
      your going out and your coming in
      from this time forth and for ever more.

Psalms 121:5–8

46 Out of the depths I cry to thee, O Lord!
      Lord, hear my voice!
      Let thy ears be attentive
        to the voice of my supplications!

Psalms 130:1–2

47 If thou, O Lord, shouldst mark iniquities,
      Lord, who could stand?
    But there is forgiveness with thee,
      that thou mayest be feared.
    I wait for the Lord, my soul waits,
      and in his word I hope.

Psalms 130:3–5

48 I will extol thee, my God and King,
      and bless thy name for ever and ever.

Psalms 145:1

49   Every day I will bless thee,
      and praise thy name for ever and ever.
    Great is the Lord, and greatly to be praised,
      and his greatness is unsearchable.

Psalms 145:2–3

50   The Lord is gracious and merciful,
      slow to anger and abounding in steadfast love.
    The Lord is good to all,
      and his compassion is over all that he has made.

Psalms 145:8–9

51   They shall speak of the glory of thy kingdom,
      and tell of thy power,
    to make known to the sons of men thy mighty deeds,
      and the glorious splendor of thy kingdom.
    Thy kingdom is an everlasting kingdom.
      and thy dominion endures throughout all generations.

Psalms 145:11–13

52   The Lord upholds all who are falling,
      and raises up all who are bowed down.

Psalms 145:14

53   The Lord is near to all who call upon him,
      to all who call upon him in truth.
    He fulfils the desire of all who fear him,
      he also hears their cry, and saves them.

Psalms 145:18–19

54   O Lord, thou art my God;
    I will exalt thee, I will praise thy name;
      for thou hast done wonderful things,
      plans formed of old, faithful and sure.

Isaiah 25:1

55   For thus said the Lord God, the Holy One of Israel
    "In returning and rest you shall be saved;
      in quietness and in trust shall be your strength."

Isaiah 30:15

56   I know the plans I have for you, says the Lord, plans for welfare and not for evil, to give you a future and a hope. Then you will call upon me and come and pray to me, and I will hear you. You will seek me and find me; when you seek me with all your heart.

Jeremiah 29:11–13

57   It is good that one should wait quietly for the salvation of the Lord.

Lamentations 3:26

58   Let us test and examine our ways,
        and return to the Lord!
    Let us lift up our hearts and hands
        to God in heaven.

Lamentations 3:40–41

59   Yet even now, says the Lord,
        return to me with all your heart,
    with fasting, with weeping, and with mourning;
        and rend your hearts and not your garments.
    Return to the Lord, your God,
        for he is gracious and merciful,
    slow to anger, and abounding in steadfast love.

Joel 2:12–13

60   Let us go at once to entreat the favor of the Lord,
        and to seek the Lord of hosts; I am going.

Zechariah 9:21

B.   FROM THE NEW TESTAMENT

61   Ask, and it will be given you; seek and you will find; knock, and it will be opened to you. For every one who asks receives, and he who seeks finds, and to him who knocks it will be opened.

Matthew 7:7–8

62   Not every one who says to me, "Lord, Lord," shall enter the kingdom of heaven, but he who does the will of my Father who is in heaven.

Matthew 7:21

63 If two of you agree on earth about anything they ask, it will be done for them by my Father in heaven. For where two or three are gathered in my name, there am I in the midst of them.

Matthew 18:19–20

64 For he who is mighty has done great things for me,
and holy is his name.

Luke 1:49

65 And he told them a parable, to tne effect that they ought always to pray and not lose heart.

Luke 18:1

66 The hour is coming, and now is, when the true worshippers will worship the Father in spirit and truth, for such the Father seeks to worship him. God is spirit and those who worship him must worship in spirit and truth.

John 4:23–24

67 Whatever you ask in my name, I will do it, that the Father may be glorified in the Son; if you ask anything in my name, I will do it.

John 14:13–14

68 For everyone who calls upon the name of the Lord will be saved.

Romans 10:13

69 Blessed be the God and Father of our Lord Jesus Christ, the Father of mercies and God of all comfort, who comforts us in all our affliction, so that we may be able to comfort those who are in any affliction, with the comfort with which we ourselves are comforted by God.

II Corinthians 1:3–4

70 Such is the confidence that we have through Christ toward God. Not that we are sufficient of ourselves to claim anything as coming from us; our sufficiency is from God.

II Corinthians 3:4–5

71 Blessed be the God and Father of our Lord Jesus Christ, who has blessed us in Christ with every spiritual blessing in the heavenly places.

Ephesians 1:3

72   Now to him who by the power at work within us is able to do far more abundantly than all that we ask or think, to him be glory in the church and in Christ Jesus to all generations, for ever and ever.

Ephesians 3:20–21

73   In everything by prayer and supplication with thanksgiving let your requests be made known to God. And the peace of God, which passes all understanding, will keep your hearts and your minds in Christ Jesus.

Philippians 4:6–7

74   God will supply every need of yours according to his riches in glory in Christ Jesus. To our God and Father be glory for ever and ever. Amen.

Philippians 4:19–20

75   Continue steadfastly in prayer, being watchful in it with thanksgiving.

Colossians 4:2

76   First of all, then, I urge that supplications, prayers, intercessions, and thanksgivings be made for all men, for kings and all who are in high positions, that we may lead a quiet and peaceable life, godly and respectful in every way. This is good, and it is acceptable in the sight of God our Savior, who desires all men to be saved and to come to the knowledge of the truth.

I Timothy 2:1–4

77   Let us then with confidence draw near to the throne of grace, that we may receive mercy and find grace to help in time of need.

Hebrews 4:16

78   Therefore, brethren, since we have confidence to enter the sanctuary by the blood of Jesus . . . let us draw near with a true heart in full assurance of faith . . . let us hold fast the confession of our hope without wavering, for he who promised is faithful.

Hebrews 10:19, 22–23

79   If any of you lacks wisdom, let him ask God who gives to all men generously and without reproaching, and it will be given him.

James 1:5

80   Submit yourselves therefore to God. Draw near to God and he will draw near to you.

James 4:7–8

81   Humble yourselves before the Lord and he will exalt you.

James 4:10

82   Humble yourselves therefore under the mighty hand of God, that in due time he may exalt you.

I Peter 5:6

83   The God of all grace, who has called you to his eternal glory in Christ, will himself restore, establish, and strengthen you. To him be the dominion for ever and ever. Amen.

I Peter 5:10–11

84   If we say we have no sin, we deceive ourselves, and the truth is not in us. If we confess our sins, he is faithful and just, and will forgive our sins and cleanse us from all unrighteousness.

I John 1:8–9

85   See what love the Father has given us, that we should be called children of God.

I John 3:1

86   This is the confidence which we have in him, that if we ask anything according to his will he hears us. And if we know that he hears us in whatever we ask, we know that we have obtained the requests made of him.

I John 5:14–15

87   Behold, I stand at the door and knock; if any one hears my voice and opens the door, I will come in to him and eat with him, and he with me.

Revelation 3:20

C. FROM OTHER SOURCES

88   Let us bow not only our heads, but our wills to God in prayer.

89   Silently now we wait for Thee,
      Ready, our God, Thy will to see.
      Open our eyes that we may see
      Glimpses of truth we have from Thee.

Clara H. Scott, 1896

90   The things, good Lord, that we pray for, give us grace to labor for; through Jesus Christ our Lord.

Thomas Moore, 1779–1852

91   To whom shall we flee for help? Our help is in the name of the Lord who made heaven and earth. Unto him let us lift our hearts in prayer.

92   It is a good thing to give thanks unto the Lord, and to sing praises unto the name of the Most High. Let us offer unto Him the sacrifice of thanksgiving.

93   In His will is our peace.

Dante, 1265–1321

94   I exhort you, says the Apostle, that supplications, prayers, intercessions, and thanksgivings be made for all men, for this is good and acceptable in the sight of God our Savior. Let us pray.

95   A single grateful thought towards heaven is the most complete prayer.

Gotthold Ephraim Lessing, 1729–1781

96   Take time to be holy,
      Speak oft with thy Lord,
      Abide with Him always
      And feed on his Word.

W. D. Longstaff, 1822–1894

97   Thou hast made us for Thyself, and our hearts are restless until they repose in Thee.

St. Augustine, 354–430

98   Let us with one heart and one voice humbly confess our sins to Almighty God, our heavenly Father.

99   Let us lift up our hearts in praise and in thanksgiving unto God.

100   Sweet hour of prayer! Sweet hour of prayer
That calls us from a world of care,
And bids us at our Father's throne,
Make all our wants and wishes known;
In seasons of distress and grief,
Our souls have often found relief;
And oft escaped the tempter's snare,
By thy return, sweet hour of prayer.
William W. Walford

101   The Lord is good to all, and His tender mercies are over all His works. The Lord upholdeth all that fall and raiseth up all that be bowed down; and not one of His creatures is forgotten before God.

102   Know this: That you are not able to do these things of yourself, nor to walk in the commandments of God, and to serve Him, without his special grace: which you must learn at all times to call by diligent prayer.
Book of Common Prayer, U.S.A.

103   There is a place of quiet rest
Near to the heart of God.
A place where sin cannot molest
Near to the heart of God.
Cleland B. McAfee, 1866–1944

104   Prayer is the most perfect and most divine action that a rational soul is capable of. It is of all other actions and duties the most indispensably necessary.
Augustin Baker, O.S.B., 1575–1641

105   Give me (us) the serenity to accept the things which cannot be changed, the courage to change those things which can be, and the wisdom to distinguish one from the other.
Reinhold Niebuhr

106   Great God, to whom since time began
      The world has prayed and striven;
      Maker of stars, and earth, and man,
      To Thee our praise is given.
      Of suns Thou art the Sun,
      Eternal, holy One;
      Who us can help, save Thou?
      To Thee alone we bow;
      Hear us, O God in heaven!

107   Teach us to pray often; that we may pray oftener.

108   I will therefore that men pray everywhere lifting up holy hands without wrath or disputing.

109   Lord, what a change within us one short hour
      Spent in Thy presence will prevail to make!
      What heavy burdens from our bosoms take,
      What parched grounds refresh as with a shower!
      We kneel, and all around us seems to lower;
      We rise, and all, the distant and near,
      Stands forth in sunny outline brave and clear;
      We kneel, how weak! we rise, how full of power!
      Why, therefore, should we do ourselves this wrong,
      Or others, that we are not always strong,
      That we are sometimes overborne with care,
      That we should ever weak or heartless be,
      Anxious or troubled, when with us is prayer,
      And joy and strength and courage are with Thee!
          Archbishop Richard Chenevix Trench, 1807–1886

110   Prayer is the peace of our spirit, the stillness of our thoughts, the evenness of recollection, the seat of meditation, the rest of our cares, and the calm of our tempest; prayer is the issue of a quiet mind, of untroubled thoughts, it is the daughter of charity and the sister of meekness.
          Jeremy Taylor, 1613–1667

111   Drop Thy still dews of quietness
        Till all our strivings cease;
      Take from our souls the strain and stress,
      And let our ordered lives confess
        The beauty of Thy peace.
          John Greenleaf Whittier, 1807–1892

112   Let no unworthy thought
Enter thy musing mind;
Things which the world hath wrought
Untrue, unclean, unkind,
Leave these behind.

Donald Cox

113   God warms his hands at man's heart when he prays.

John Masefield, 1875–1960

114   Come, let us fall upon our knees before the great God of Israel, creator of heaven and earth, father of poor and rich, of small and great, of slave and lord—the mighty God who has shown us His mighty hand and His outstretched arm.

Sholem Asch

115   More things are wrought by prayer
Than this world dreams of. Wherefore, let thy voice
Rise like a fountain for me night and day.
For what are men better than sheep and goats
That nourish a blind life within the brain,
If, knowing God, they lift not hands of prayer
Both for themselves and those who call them friend?
For so the whole round earth is every way
Bound by gold chains about the feet of God.

Alfred Lord Tennyson, 1808–1892

116   Breathe on me, Breath of God, Fill me with life anew,
That I may love what Thou dost love, and do what
    Thou wouldst do.
Breathe on me, Breath of God, until my heart is pure,
Until with Thee I will one will, to do and to endure.

Edwin Hatch, 1835–1899

117   Prayer unites the soul to God. For though the soul be ever like to God in nature and substance, restored by grace, it is often unlike in condition by sin on man's part. Then is prayer a witness that the soul wills as God wills, and it comforts the conscience and enables man to grace. And so He teaches us to pray and mightily trusts that we shall have it. For He beholdeth us in love and would make us partners of His good deed. And therefore He moves us to pray for that which it pleases Him to do.

Julian of Norwich, 14th Century

118   Lord, we know not what is good for us. Thou knowest what it is. For it we pray.

India

119   When you pray, endeavor to pray more for others than for yourself alone. Pray for all as you would pray for yourself, with the same sincerity and fervor; look upon their infirmities and sicknesses as your own, their sins and passions as your own, their temptations, misfortunes, and manifold afflictions as your own. Such prayer will be accepted with great favor by the heavenly Father.

John of Cronstadt, 1829–1908

120   Remember that God commandeth thee by prayer to call upon Him for remedy, aid, and help, saying: Ask, seek, knock; watch and pray; call upon me in the day of tribulation.

121   Consider that God doth not only command thee to pray, but also promiseth graciously to hear and grant all thine honest, lawful, and godly requests and petitions.

122   Thou must never ask for worldly and corruptible things, pertaining to this transitory life, such as bodily health, wealth, or strength, without employing in thy prayer such conditions as these, "if it be Thy will, O Lord;" "if it be for my soul's health, profit and advantage; if not, Thy will be done, not mine."

123   Thou must not appoint any certain time to God for granting thy requests; but utterly commit that to His Godly will and pleasure, who knoweth best what time of granting thy requests is most commodious and profitable for thee.

124   Ask things pertaining to thy salvation, remission of sin, and life everlasting, without condition. For these hath God certainly promised to all them that with a true, faithful, and obedient heart do come unto Him in earnest and continued prayer.

125   Dearly beloved, the heavenly Father in whose presence we now stand is always more than ready to hear us pray; nor does anything hide him from us but the veil of our impure and earthly mind. And since the preparations of

even the willing heart are not without him, let us inwardly pray for the grace of a humble and holy spirit, that for a little while we may be alone with him; and as his beloved Son went up into the mountain to pray, so we may rise above the haste and press of life, and commune with him in spirit and in truth.

James Martineau, 1805–1900

126   Dearly beloved brethren, the Scripture moveth us in sundry places to acknowledge and confess our manifold sins and wickedness; and that we should not dissemble nor cloak them before the face of Almighty God our Heavenly Father; but confess them with an humble, lowly, penitent, and obedient heart; to the end that we may obtain forgiveness of the same by his infinite goodness and mercy . . . We should not be careless concerning the necessities of our bodies or souls . . . Wherefore I pray and beseech you as many as are here present to accompany me with a pure heart, and humble voice, unto the throne of the heavenly grace.

Book of Common Prayer

127   Minister: O Lord, open Thou our lips
   People: And our mouth shall show forth Thy praise.

   Minister: Praise ye the Lord.
   People: The Lord's name be praised.

   Minister: The Lord be with you
   People: And with thy spirit

   Minister: Let us pray.

Devotional Services

VII

Words
of
Assurance
and
Forgiveness

A. FROM SCRIPTURE

1   The eternal God is your dwelling place, and underneath are the everlasting arms.

Deuteronomy 33:27

2   Have I not commanded you? Be strong and of good courage; be not frightened, neither be dismayed; for the Lord your God is with you wherever you go.

Joshua 1:9

3   If my people who are called by my name humble themselves, and pray and seek my face, and turn from their wicked ways, then I will hear from heaven, and will forgive their sin and heal their land.

II Chronicles 7:14

4   For the Lord your God is gracious and merciful, and will not turn away his face from you, if you return to him.

II Chronicles 30:9

5   Thou art a God ready to forgive, gracious and merciful, slow to anger and abounding in steadfast love.

Nehemiah 9:17

6   Sing praises to the Lord, O you his saints,
    and give thanks to his holy name.
For his anger is but for a moment,
    and his favor is for a lifetime.
Weeping may tarry for the night,
    but joy comes with the morning.

Psalms 30:4–5

7   When the righteous cry for help, the Lord hears,
    and delivers them out of all their troubles.
The Lord is near to the brokenhearted,
    and saves the crushed in spirit.

Psalms 34:17–18

8   How precious is thy steadfast love, O God!
      The children of men take refuge in the shadow of
        thy wings.
   They feast on the abundance of thy house,
      and thou givest them drink from the river of thy
        delights.
   For with thee is the fountain of life;
      in thy light do we see light.

Psalms 36:7–9

9   Purge me with hyssop, and I shall be clean;
      wash me, and I shall be whiter than snow.

Psalms 51:7

10   The sacrifice acceptable to God is a broken spirit,
      a broken and contrite heart, O God, thou wilt not
       despise.

Psalms 51:17

11   Help us, O God of our salvation,
      for the glory of thy name;
   deliver us, and forgive our sins,
      for thy name's sake!

Psalms 79:9

12   But thou, O Lord, art a God merciful and gracious,
      slow to anger and abounding in steadfast love and
       faithfulness.

Psalms 86:15

13   The Lord is merciful and gracious,
      slow to anger and abounding in steadfast love.
   He will not always chide,
      nor will he keep his anger for ever.
   He does not deal with us according to our sins,
      nor requite us according to our iniquities.
   For as the heavens are high above the earth,
      so great is his steadfast love toward those who fear
       him;
      as far as the east is from the west,
      so far does he remove our transgressions from us.

Psalms 103:8–12

14   The Lord is gracious and merciful,
      slow to anger and abounding in steadfast love.
  The Lord is good to all,
      and his compassion is over all that he has made.
Psalms 145:8–9

15   The Lord is near to all who call upon him,
      to all who call upon him in truth.
  He fulfils the desire of all who fear him,
      he also hears their cry, and saves them.
Psalms 145:18–19

16   I, I am He
      who blots out your transgressions for my own sake,
      and I will not remember your sins.
Isaiah 43:25

17   Let the wicked forsake his way,
      and the unrighteous man his thoughts;
  let him return to the Lord, that he may have mercy
      on him,
      and to our God, for he will abundantly pardon.
Isaiah 55:7

18   The steadfast love of the Lord never ceases,
      his mercies never come to an end;
  They are new every morning;
      great is thy faithfulness.
Lamentations 3:22–23

19   Take heart, my son, your sins are forgiven.
Matthew 9:2

20   Come to me, all who labor and are heavy-laden, and I will give you rest. Take my yoke upon you, and learn from me; for I am gentle and lowly in heart, and you will find rest for your souls. For my yoke is easy, and my burden is light.
Matthew 11:28–30

21   And whenever you stand praying, forgive, if you have anything against any one; so that your Father also who is in heaven may forgive you your trespasses.
Mark 11:25

22 For God so loved the world that he gave his only Son, that whoever believes in him should not perish but have eternal life.

John 3:16

23 God, be merciful to me a sinner!

Luke 18:13

24 Him who comes to me I will not cast out. For this is the will of my Father, that every one who sees the Son and believes in him should have eternal life.

John 6:37, 40

25 Since we are justified by faith, we have peace with God through our Lord Jesus Christ.

Romans 5:1

26 For the wages of sin is death, but the free gift of God is eternal life in Christ Jesus our Lord.

Romans 6:23

27 There is therefore now no condemnation for those who are in Christ Jesus.

Romans 8:1

28 If God is for us, who is against us? He who did not spare his own Son but gave him up for us all, will he not also give us all things with him?

Romans 8:31–32

29 No temptation has overtaken you that is not common to man. God is faithful, and he will not let you be tempted beyond your strength, but with the temptation will also provide the way of escape, that you may be able to endure it.

I Corinthians 10:13

30 Now may our Lord Jesus Christ himself, and God our Father, who loved us and gave us eternal comfort and good hope through grace, comfort your hearts and establish them in every good work and word.

II Thessalonians 2:16–17

31 The saying is sure and worthy of full acceptance, that Christ Jesus came into the world to save sinners.

I Timothy 1:15

32   God is not so unjust as to overlook your work and the love which you showed for his sake in serving the saints, as you still do.

Hebrews 6:10

33   This is the message we have heard from him and proclaim to you, that God is light and in him is no darkness at all. If we walk in the light, as he is in the light, we have fellowship with one another, and the blood of Jesus his Son cleanses us from all sin.

I John 1:5, 7

34   If we say we have no sin, we deceive ourselves and the truth is not in us. If we confess our sins, he is faithful and just, and will forgive our sins and cleanse us from all unrighteousness.

I John 1:8–9

35   My little children, I am writing this to you so that you may not sin; but if any one does sin, we have an advocate with the Father, Jesus Christ the righteous; and he is the expiation for our sins, and not for ours only but also for the sins of the whole world.

I John 2:1–2

B.   FROM OTHER SOURCES

36   Hear what comfortable words our Saviour Christ saith unto all that truly turn to him: Come unto me, all ye that labor and are heavy laden, and I will give you rest.

Hear also the words from St. John's Gospel: God so loved the world, that he gave his only begotten Son that whosoever believeth in him should not perish, but have everlasting life.

Hear also these words of Scripture: The Lord is gracious, and full of compassion; slow to anger, and of great mercy.

The sacrifices of God are a broken spirit; a broken and a contrite heart, O God, thou wilt not despise.

As the heaven is high above the earth, so great is his mercy toward them that fear him.

As far as the east is from the west, so far hath he removed our transgressions from us.

Like as a father pitieth his children, so the Lord pitieth them that fear him.

If we confess our sins, he is faithful and just to forgive us our sins, and to cleanse us from all unrighteousness.

This is a faithful saying, and worthy of all acceptation, that Christ Jesus came into the world to save sinners.

There is therefore now no condemnation to them who are in Christ Jesus, who walk not after the flesh, but after the Spirit.

This is the message which we have heard of him, and declare unto you, that God is light, and in him is no darkness at all. If we walk in the light, as he is in the light, we have fellowship one with another, and the blood of Jesus Christ his Son cleanseth us from all sin.

The Lord is my light and my salvation; whom shall I fear? the Lord is the strength of my life; of whom shall I be afraid?

In the time of trouble he shall hide me in his pavilion: in the secret of his tabernacle shall he hide me.

Wait on the Lord: be of good courage, and he shall strengthen thine heart: wait, I say, on the Lord.

The Lord is nigh unto them that are of a broken heart; and saveth such as be of a contrite spirit.

The Lord redeemeth the soul of his servants: and none of them that trust in him shall be desolate.

Trust in the Lord; wait patiently for him; and he shall give thee the desires of thine heart.

Jesus said: Him that cometh to me I will in no wise cast out.

My God shall supply all your need according to his riches in glory by Christ Jesus.

Ask and it shall be given you; seek . . . knock . . . for everyone that asketh . . . etc.

The Book of Worship

37 This is the assurance we have in God, that, if we ask according to His will, He heareth us.

38 God so loved the world, that he gave his only begotten Son, that whosoever believeth in him should not perish, but have everlasting life. Hear the gracious words of our Lord Jesus Christ unto all that truly repent and turn to him; Come unto me, all ye that labor and are heavy laden, and I will give you rest. Him that cometh to me I will in no wise cast out.

39 Come now, and let us reason together, said the Lord; though your sins be as scarlet, they shall be as white as snow; though they be red like crimson, they shall be as wool. If thou, Lord, shouldest mark iniquities, O Lord, who shall stand? But there is forgiveness with thee. Hope in the Lord; for with the Lord there is mercy, and with him is plenteous redemption.

40 As far as east is distant from the west, so far hath he from us removed in his love all our iniquity. Such pity as a Father hath unto his children dear, hath he to us who often fail, who yet would serve him here.

VIII

Prayers
of
Confession
and
Pardon

---

1 Our Heavenly Father, thou hast assured us that if we confess our sins, thou art faithful and just to forgive our sins and to cleanse us from all unrighteousness. Give us true penitence, and help us unfeignedly to believe thy power and pardon. Cleanse our hearts and renew right spirits within us, and give us the peace and joy of thy forgiveness, as gratefully we look up to thee. In Christ's name we ask it.

Book of Common Worship

2 The Almighty and merciful God, grant unto us, being penitent, pardon and remission of all our sins, time for amendment of life, and the grace and comfort of His Holy Spirit.

Service Book and Hymnal

3 Blessed by Thy name, O Lord, that, according to the comforting assurance of Thy word, Thou dost forgive the sins of all who truly repent, who believe in the Lord Jesus Christ, and are resolved to walk in newness of life. Grant, we beseech Thee, to all such here present the full assurance of pardon and reconciliation, and the peace which passeth all understanding; through Jesus Christ our Lord.

Book of Common Order

4 May Almighty God who doth freely pardon all who repent and turn to Him, now fulfill in every contrite heart the promise of redeeming grace; remitting all our sins, and cleansing us from an evil conscience; through the perfect sacrifice of Christ Jesus our Lord.

Henry Van Dyke, 1852–1933

5 O God, whose nature and property is ever to have mercy and to forgive, receive our humble petitions; and let the overwhelming boundlessness of thy great mercy loose us from our sins.

Book of Common Worship

6 Almighty God, the Father of our Lord Jesus Christ, who desirest not the death of a sinner, but rather that he may turn from his wickedness and live; have mercy upon all here present who repent and turn to Thee; grant unto them full remission and forgiveness; absolve them from all

their sins, iniquities and transgressions, and vouchsafe unto them Thy Holy Spirit.

Book of Common Order

7 Grant that as many here present as truly repent of their sins, and believe in the Lord Jesus Christ with full purpose of new obedience, may now receive with perfect faith the declaration made by the authority and in the name of Christ, that their sins are forgiven in heaven, according to His promise in the Gospel, through Jesus Christ our Saviour.

8 O Lord God, there is none like unto thee, in the heavens or upon the earth; yet hast thou promised to hear the cry of those who call upon thee; wherefore have respect unto the supplications of thy servants, and hearken unto the prayer that they make before thee; and howsoever they may have sinned, yet hear thou in heaven thy dwelling place, and when thou hearest, Lord, forgive.

The Book of Worship

9 Almighty God, our Heavenly Father, who of thy great mercy hast promised forgiveness of sins to all them that with hearty repentance and true faith turn unto thee, have mercy upon us; pardon and deliver us from all our sins; confirm and strengthen us in all goodness; and bring us to everlasting life.

Book of Common Worship

10 Almighty God, who doth freely pardon all who repent and turn to thee, fulfill in every contrite heart the promise of redeeming grace; forgive all our sins, and cleanse us from an evil conscience through Jesus Christ our Lord.

11 Almighty and everlasting God, who art always more ready to hear than we to pray, and art wont to give more than either we desire or deserve, pour down upon us the abundance of thy mercy, forgiving us those things whereof our conscience is afraid, and giving us those good things which we are not worthy to ask, but through the merits and mediation of Jesus Christ, thy Son, our Lord.

The Book of Common Prayer

123

12   O Lord, we beseech thee, pardon and absolve thy people from their offences; that, through thy bountiful goodness, we may be delivered from the bonds of those sins which by our frailty we have committed. Grant this, O heavenly Father, for Jesus Christ's sake, our adorable Lord and Saviour.

Book of Common Worship

13   Almighty God, and most merciful Father, who delightest not in the death of a sinner, but rather that he be converted from his sin and live: give unto Thy servants a deep contrition for their sins, a perfect hatred, and a full remission of them.

Book of Common Order

14   Almighty God have mercy upon you, forgive you all your sins, and deliver you from all evil, comfort and strengthen you in all goodness, and bring you to life everlasting.

The Scottish Book of Common Prayer

15   May the Almighty and merciful Lord grant unto you pardon and remission of all your sins, time for amendment of life, and the grace and comfort of the Holy Spirit.

The Prayer Book as proposed in 1928

16   Grant, we beseech Thee, merciful Lord, to thy faithful people, pardon and peace, that they may be cleansed from all their sins and serve Thee with a quiet mind; through Jesus Christ our Lord.

Book of Common Order

17   Gracious God and Father of our Lord Jesus Christ, have mercy upon Thy servants who bow before Thee; pardon and forgive us all our sins.

18   Almighty God, the Father of our Lord Jesus Christ, who desirest not the death of a sinner, but rather that he may turn from his wickedness and live; thou dost pardon and absolve all them that truly repent and unfeignedly believe thy holy gospel. Wherefore we beseech thee to grant us true repentance, and thy Holy Spirit, that those things may please thee which we do at this present, and that the rest of

our living hereafter may be pure and holy, so that at the last we may come to eternal joy, through Jesus Christ our Lord.

The Book of Worship

19   O God, who art faithful and just to forgive us our sins; mercifully grant that we may be delivered from the bondage of our sins and may one day rejoice in perfect liberty in our fatherland, which is in heaven.

Roman Breviary

20   Almighty and most merciful Father: We have erred, and strayed from thy ways like lost sheep. We have followed too much the devices and desires of our own hearts. We have offended against thy holy laws. We have left undone those things which we ought to have done; And we have done those things which we ought not to have done; And there is no health in us. But thou, O Lord, have mercy upon us, miserable offenders. Spare thou those, O God, who confess their faults. Restore thou those who are penitent; According to thy promises declared unto mankind In Christ Jesus our Lord. And grant, O most merciful Father, for his sake; That we may hereafter live a godly, righteous, and sober life, to the glory of thy holy Name. Amen.

The Book of Common Prayer

21   O Lord, be gracious unto us! In all that we hear or see, in all that we say or do, be gracious unto us.

Bedouin Prayer

22   Forgive me my sins, O Lord; forgive us the sins of our youth and the sins of our age, the sins of our soul and the sins of our body, our secret and our whispering sins, the sins we have done to please ourselves and the sins we have done to please others. Forgive those sins which we know, and the sins which we know not; forgive us, O Lord, forgive them all, of Thy great goodness.

Anonymous, 17th Century

23   O Lord, we beseech thee, mercifully hear our prayers, and spare all those who confess their sins unto thee; that they, whose consciences by sin are accused, by thy merciful pardon may be absolved; through Christ our Lord.

The Book of Common Prayer

24 Almighty God . . . have mercy upon you; pardon and deliver you from all your sins, confirm and strengthen you in all goodness, and bring you to everlasting life; through Jesus Christ our Lord.

The Book of Common Prayer, adapted

25 Grant, O Lord, that whosoever shall confess their sins and offer up their prayers and praises unto thy divine majesty in this place, may be kept from all worldly and wandering thoughts, and may draw near unto thee with such steadfastness of faith and devout affection of mind, that they may be graciously accepted in thy sight. O Lord, pardon their sins, compassionate their infirmities, enlighten and sanctify them by thy Holy Spirit, and enable them so to serve and worship thee here below, that finally they may be received into thy presence, to praise and glorify thee for evermore.

The Book of Common Prayer, Canada

26 O Lord, we beseech thee, forgive us our offenses, that through thy bountiful goodness we may be delivered from the bonds of those sins which we have committed. Grant this, O heavenly Father, for Jesus Christ's sake, our blessed Lord and Saviour.

27 May Almighty God, who caused light to shine out of darkness, shine in our hearts, cleansing us from all our sins, and restoring us to the light of the knowledge of this glory in the face of Jesus Christ our Lord.

28 Now let us be comforted and be glad, and receive the assurance of pardon given to all who repent and believe.

This is a faithful saying, and worthy of all acceptation, that Jesus Christ came into the world to save sinners.

29 May the almighty and merciful God grant us pardon, forgiveness, and remission of our sins, through Jesus Christ our Lord.

30 If we say that we have no sin, we deceive ourselves, and the truth is not in us. If we confess our sins, He is faith-

ful and just to forgive us our sins, and to cleanse us from all unrighteousness. Let us therefore confess our sins unto God, and humbly beseech Him, in the name of our Lord Jesus Christ, to grant us forgiveness, saying:

Almighty God, our Maker and Redeemer, we poor sinners confess unto Thee that we are by nature sinful and unclean, and that we have sinned against Thee by thought, word and deed. Wherefore, we flee for refuge to Thine infinite mercy, seeking and imploring Thy grace, for the sake of our Lord Jesus Christ.

Evangelical Book of Worship

31   Be pleased to shed abroad Thy love in our hearts by the Holy Ghost, and to seal unto us, by the same spirit of adoption, the full assurance of pardon and reconciliation with Thee.

The Book of Common Order, Scotland

32   May God, whose mercy droppeth as the gentle rain from heaven, forgive your sins, strengthen you in all goodness, and bring you to everlasting life.

33   The Holy Scriptures declare that when the wicked man turneth away from his wickedness and doeth that which is lawful and right, he shall save his soul and live. The sacrifices of God are a broken and a contrite heart. To the Lord belong mercy and forgiveness, though we have rebelled against Him.

Let us therefore with sincere, humble and obedient hearts, confess our sins unto our Father, that we may obtain remission of the same, by His infinite goodness and mercy, saying:

The Almighty God, our heavenly Father, who of His great mercy hath promised forgiveness of sins to all those who with hearty repentance and true faith turn unto Him, have mercy upon us; pardon and deliver us from all our sins; confirm and strengthen us in all goodness, and bring us to everlasting life.

34   Assurance of Pardon:

Minister:	Search me, O God, and know my heart
People:	Try me and know my thoughts;
Minister:	And see if there be an wicked way in me,
People:	And lead me in the way everlasting.
Minister:	Lord, lift thou up the light of thy countenance upon us.
People:	Out of the depths have I cried unto thee, O Lord.
Minister:	Lord, hear my voice:
People:	Let thine ears be attentive to the voice of my supplications.
Minister:	If thou, Lord, shouldst mark iniquities, O Lord, who could stand?
People:	But with thee there is forgiveness that thou mayest be feared.
All:	I wait for the Lord, my soul doth wait, And in his word do I hope.

The Book of Worship

IX

Offertory
Sentences

A. FROM THE OLD TESTAMENT

1   Of all that thou givest me I will give the tenth to thee.
Genesis 28:22

2   The Lord said, "Speak to the people . . . that they take for me an offering; from every man whose heart makes him willing you shall receive the offering for me."
Exodus 25:1–2

3   And you shall take the atonement money from the people of Israel, and shall appoint it for the service of the tent of meeting; that it may bring the people of Israel to remembrance before the Lord, so as to make atonement for yourselves.
Exodus 30:16

4   This is the thing which the Lord has commanded. Take from among you an offering to the Lord; whoever is of a generous heart, let him bring the Lord's offering.
Exodus 35:4–5

5   Let every able man among you come and make (give) all that the Lord has commanded.
Exodus 35:10

6   And they came, every one whose heart stirred him, and every one whose spirit moved him, and brought the Lord's offering.
Exodus 35:21

7   All the men and women, the people of Israel, whose heart moved them to bring anything for the work which the Lord had commanded by Moses to be done, brought it as their freewill offering to the Lord.
Exodus 35:29

8   If your brother becomes poor, and cannot maintain himself with you, you shall maintain him; as a stranger and a sojourner he shall live with you.
Leviticus 25:35

9   All the tithe of the land whether of the seed of the land or the fruit of the trees, is the Lord's; it is holy to the Lord.

Leviticus 27:30

10   Beware lest you say in your heart, "My power and the might of my hand have gotten me this wealth." You shall remember the Lord your God, for it is he who gives you power to get wealth.

Deuteronomy 8:17–18

11   You shall tithe all the yield of your seed, which comes forth from the field year by year.

Deuteronomy 14:22

12   If there is among you a poor man, one of your brethren, in any of your towns within your land which the Lord your God gives you, you shall not harden your heart or shut your hand against your poor brother, but you shall open your hand to him, and lend him sufficient for his need, whatever it may be.

Deuteronomy 15:7–8

13   You shall give . . . freely and your heart shall not be grudging when you give . . . because for this the Lord your God will bless you in all your work and in all that you undertake.

Deuteronomy 15:10

14   For the poor will never cease out of the land; therefore I command you, you shall open wide your hand to your brother, to the needy and to the poor, in the land.

Deuteronomy 15:11

15   You shall not appear before the Lord empty-handed.

Deuteronomy 16:16

16   Every man shall give as he is able, according to the blessing of the Lord your God which he has given you.

Deuteronomy 16:17

17   Then the priest shall take the basket from your hand, and set it down before the altar of the Lord your God, and you shall make response before the Lord your God.

Deuteronomy 26:4–5

18   David said, "Moreover, in addition to all that I have provided for the holy house, I have a treasure of my own of gold and silver, and because of my devotion to the house of my God I give it to the house of my God."

I Chronicles 29:3

19   Ascribe to the Lord, O families of the peoples,
          ascribe to the Lord glory and strength!
    Ascribe to the Lord the glory due his name;
          bring an offering, and come before him!

I Chronicles 16:28–29

20   Thine, O Lord, is the greatness, and the power, and the glory, and the victory, and the majesty; for all that is in the heavens and in the earth is thine; thine is the kingdom, O Lord, and thou art exalted as head above all.

I Chronicles 29:11

21   Both riches and honor come from thee, and thou rulest over all. In thy hand are power and might; and in thy hand it is to make great and to give strength to all. And now we thank thee, our God, and praise thy glorious name.

I Chronicles 29:12–13

22   All things come from thee, and of thy own have we given thee.

I Chronicles 29:14

23   Give thanks to the Lord,
          for his steadfast love endures for ever.

II Chronicles 20:21

24   All that a man has he will give for his life.

Job 2:4

25   Offer right sacrifices,
          and put your trust in the Lord.

Psalms 4:5

26   The earth is the Lord's and the fulness thereof,
          the world and those who dwell therein.

Psalms 24:1

27 Thou hast multiplied, O Lord my God, thy
 wondrous deeds and thy thoughts toward us;
 none can compare with thee!
Were I to proclaim and tell of them,
 they would be more than can be numbered.

          Psalms 40:5

28 Blessed is he who considers the poor!
 the Lord delivers him in the day of trouble;
the Lord protects him and keeps him alive;
 he is called blessed in the land.

         Psalms 41:1–2

29 Offer to God a sacrifice of thanksgiving,
 and pay your vows to the Most High.

          Psalms 50:14

30 With a free-will offering I will sacrifice to thee;
 I will give thanks to thy name, O Lord, for it is
 good.

          Psalms 54:6

31 Give justice to the weak and the fatherless;
 maintain the right of the afflicted and the destitute.

         Psalms 82:3

32 It is good to give thanks to the Lord,
 to sing praises to thy name, O Most High.

         Psalms 92:1

33 Ascribe to the Lord the glory due his name;
 bring an offering, and come into his courts!

         Psalms 96:8

34 Bless the Lord, O my soul; and all that is within me
 bless his holy name!
Bless the Lord, O my soul, and forget not all his
 benefits.

         Psalms 103:1–2

35 Praise the Lord,
   I will give thanks to the Lord with my whole heart,
      in the company of the upright, in the congregation.
   Great are the works of the Lord,
      studied by all who have pleasure in them.
   Full of honor and majesty in his work,
      and his righteousness endures forever.

Psalms 111:1–3

36 What shall I render to the Lord
      for all his bounty to me? . . .
   I will pay my vows to the Lord
      in the presence of all his people.

Psalms 116:12, 14

37 Honor the Lord with your substance and with the first
fruits of all your produce.

Proverbs 3:9

38 Do not withhold good from those to whom it is due,
      when it is in your power to do it.
   Do not say to your neighbor, "Go, and come again,
      tomorrow I will give it"—when you have it with
      you.

Proverbs 3:27–28

39 He who is kind to the poor lends to the Lord, and he
   will repay him for his deed.

Proverbs 19:17

40 If your enemy is hungry, give him bread to eat; and if
   he is thirsty, give him water to drink.

Proverbs 25:21

41 Cast your bread upon the waters, for you will find it
   after many days.

Ecclesiastes 11:1

42 With what shall I come before the Lord, and bow
   myself before God on high?
   Shall I come before him with burnt offerings,
      with calves a year old?

Will the Lord be pleased with thousands of rams,
   with ten thousands of rivers of oil?
Shall I give my first-born for my transgression,
   the fruit of my body for the sin of my soul?
He has showed you, O man, what is good;
   and what does the Lord require of you
but to do justice, and to love kindness,
   and to walk humbly with your God?

Micah 6:6–8

43   Bring the full tithes into the storehouse, that there may be food in my house; and thereby put me to the test, says the Lord of hosts, if I will not open the windows of heaven for you and pour down for you an overflowing blessing.

Malachi 3:10

B. FROM THE NEW TESTAMENT

44   Then, opening their treasures, they offered him gifts, gold and frankincense and myrrh.

Matthew 2:11

45   Blessed are the merciful, for they shall obtain mercy.

Matthew 5:7

46   Let your light so shine before men, that they may see your good works and give glory to your Father who is in heaven.

Matthew 5:16

47   If you are offering your gift at the altar, and there remember that your brother has something against you, leave your gift there before the altar and go; first be reconciled to your brother, and then come and offer your gift.

Matthew 5:23–24

48   If any one forces you to go one mile, go with him two miles. Give to him who begs from you, and do not refuse him who would borrow from you.

Matthew 5:41–42

49   When you give alms, do not let your left hand know what your right hand is doing, so that your alms may be in secret; and your Father who sees in secret will reward you.

Matthew 6:3–4

50   Do not lay up for yourselves treasures on earth, where moth and rust consume and where thieves break in and steal, but lay up for yourselves treasures in heaven, where neither moth nor rust consumes and where thieves do not break in and steal. For where your treasure is, there will your heart be also.

Matthew 6:19–21

51   Seek first his kingdom and his righteousness, and all these things shall be yours as well.

Matthew 6:33

52   What man of you, if his son asks him for a loaf, will give him a stone? Or if he asks for a fish, will give him a serpent?

Matthew 7:9–10

53   Whatever you wish that men would do to you, do so to them; for this is the law and the prophets.

Matthew 7:12

54   Freely ye have received, freely give.

Matthew 10:8 KJV

55   What will it profit a man, if he gains the whole world and forfeits his life? Or what shall a man give in return for his life? . . . If any man would come after me, let him deny himself and take up his cross and follow me.

Matthew 16:26, 24

56   Jesus said to him, "If you would be perfect, go, sell what you possess and give to the poor, and you will have treasure in heaven; and come, follow me."

Matthew 19:21

57   Render therefore to Caesar the things that are Caesar's and to God the things that are God's.

Matthew 22:21

58   Jesus said, "For I was hungry and you gave me food, I was thirsty and you gave me drink, I was a stranger and you welcomed me, I was naked and you clothed me, I was sick and you visited me, I was in prison and you came to me."

Matthew 25:35–36

59   As you did it to one of the least of these my brethren, you did it to me.

Matthew 25:40

60   Take heed what you hear; the measure you give will be the measure you get, and still more will be given you. For to him who has will more be given; and from him who has not, even what he has will be taken away.

Mark 4:24–25

61   For the Son of man also came not to be served but to serve, and to give his life as a ransom for many.

Mark 10:45

62   And he sat down opposite the treasury, and watched the multitude putting money into the treasury. Many rich people put in large sums. And a poor widow came, and put in two copper coins, which make a penny. And he called his disciples to him, and said to them, "Truly, I say to you, this poor widow has put in more than all those who are contributing to the treasury. For they all contributed out of their abundance; but she out of her poverty has put in everything she had, her whole living."

Mark 12:41–44

63   Jesus said, "He who has two coats, let him share with him who has none; and he who has food, let him do likewise."

Luke 3:11

64   Love your enemies, and do good, and lend, expecting nothing in return; and your reward will be great, and you will be sons of the Most High . . . Be merciful, even as your Father is merciful.

Luke 6:35–36

65   Give, and it will be given to you; good measure, pressed down, shaken together, running over, will be put into your lap. For the measure you give will be the measure you get back.

Luke 6:38

66   If any man would come after me, let him deny himself and take up his cross daily and follow me. For whoever would save his life will lose it; and whoever loses his life for my sake, he will save it. For what does it profit a man if he gains the whole world and loses or forfeits himself?

Luke 9:23–25

67   You shall love the Lord your God with all your heart, and with all your soul, and with all your strength, and with all your mind; and your neighbor as yourself.

Luke 10:27

68   Rather give alms of such things as ye have; and behold, all things are clean unto you.

Luke 11:41

69   Take heed, and beware of all covetousness; for a man's life does not consist in the abundance of his possessions.

Luke 12:15

70   Sell your possessions, and give alms; provide yourselves with purses that do not grow old, with a treasure in the heavens that does not fail, where no thief approaches and no moth destroys. For where your treasure is, there will your heart be also.

Luke 12:33–34

71   Every one to whom much is given, of him will much be required; and of him to whom men commit much they will demand the more.

Luke 12:48

72   No servant can serve two masters; for either he will hate the one and love the other, or he will be devoted to the one and despise the other. You cannot serve God and mammon.

Luke 16:13

73 Jesus said, "One thing you still lack. Sell all that you have and distribute to the poor, and you will have treasure in heaven; and come, follow me."

Luke 18:22

74 For God so loved the world that he gave his only Son, that whoever believes in him should not perish but have eternal life.

John 3:16

75 All who believed were together and had all things in common.

Acts 2:44

76 And the disciples determined, every one according to his ability, to send relief to the brethren who lived in Judea.

Acts 11:29

77 In all things I have shown you that by so toiling one must help the weak, remembering the words of the Lord Jesus, how he said, "It is more blessed to give than to receive."

Acts 20:35

78 Having gifts that differ according to the grace given to us, let us use them: if prophecy, in proportion to our faith; if service, in our serving; he who teaches, in his teaching; he who exhorts, in his exhortation; he who contributes, in liberality; he who gives aid, with zeal; he who does acts of mercy, with cheerfulness.

Romans 12:6–8

79 Owe no one anything, except to love one another; for he who loves his neighbor has fulfilled the law.

Romans 13:8

80 The Kingdom of God does not mean food and drink but righteousness and peace and joy in the Holy Spirit.

Romans 14:17

81 We who are strong ought to bear with the failings of the weak, and not to please ourselves; let each of us please his neighbor for his good, to edify him.

Romans 15:1–2

82   It is required of stewards that they be found trustworthy.

I Corinthians 4:2

83   On the first day of every week, each of you is to put something aside and store it up, as he may prosper.

I Corinthians 16:2

84   In a severe test of affliction, their abundance of joy and their extreme poverty have overflowed in a wealth of liberality on their part.

II Corinthians 8:2

85   They gave according to their means, as I can testify and beyond their means, of their own free will . . . but first they gave themselves to the Lord.

II Corinthians 8:3–5

86   Now as you excel in everything—in faith, in utterance, in knowledge, in all earnestness, and in your love for us—see that you excel in this gracious work also.

II Corinthians 8:7

87   You know the grace of our Lord Jesus Christ, that though he was rich, yet for your sake he became poor, so that by his poverty you might become rich.

II Corinthians 8:9

88   If the readiness is there, it is acceptable according to what a man has, not according to what he has not.

II Corinthians 8:12

89   Give proof, before the churches, of your love.

II Corinthians 8:24

90   He who sows sparingly will also reap sparingly, and he who sows bountifully will also reap bountifully.

II Corinthians 9:6

91   Each one must do as he has made up his mind, not reluctantly or under compulsion, for God loves a cheerful giver.

II Corinthians 9:7

92   God is able to provide you with every blessing in abundance, so that you may always have enough of everything and may provide in abundance for every good work.

II Corinthians 9:8

93   He who supplies seed to the sower and bread for food will supply and multiply your resources and increase the harvest of your righteousness. You will be enriched in every way for great generosity, which through us will produce thanksgiving to God; for the rendering of this service not only supplies the wants of the saints but also overflows in many thanksgivings to God.

II Corinthians 9:10–12

94   Bear one another's burdens, and so fulfil the law of Christ.

Galatians 6:2

95   Let us not grow weary in well-doing, for in due season we shall reap, if we do not lose heart.

Galatians 6:9

96   As we have opportunity, let us do good to all men, and especially to those who are of the household of faith.

Galatians 6:10

97   Whatever your task, work heartily, as serving the Lord and not men.

Colossians 3:23

Whatsoever ye do, do it heartily, as to the Lord, and not unto men.

Colossians 3:23 KJV

98   But concerning love of the brethren you have no need to have any one write to you, for you yourselves have been taught by God to love one another.

I Thessalonians 4:9

99   There is great gain in godliness with contentment; for we brought nothing into the world, and we cannot take anything out of the world.

I Timothy 6:6–7

100   Those who desire to be rich fall into temptation, into a snare, into many senseless and hurtful desires that plunge men into ruin and destruction.

For the love of money is the root of all evils; it is through this craving that some have wandered away from the faith and pierced their hearts with many pangs.

I Timothy 6:9–10

101   As for the rich in this world, charge them not to be haughty, nor to set their hopes on uncertain riches but on God who richly furnishes us with everything to enjoy. They are to do good, to be rich in good deeds, liberal and generous, thus laying up for themselves a good foundation for the future, so that they may take hold of the life which is life indeed. (O Timothy,) guard what has been entrusted to you.

I Timothy 6:17–20

102   God is not so unjust as to overlook your work and the love which you showed for his sake in serving the saints, as you still do.

Hebrews 6:10

103   Through him let us continually offer up a sacrifice of praise to God.

Hebrews 13:15

104   Do not neglect to do good and to share what you have, for such sacrifices are pleasing to God.

Hebrews 13:16

105   As each has received a gift, employ it for one another, as good stewards of God's varied grace.

I Peter 4:10

Whatever gift each of you may have received, use it in service to one another, like good stewards dispensing the grace of God in its varied forms.

NEB

106   If any one has the world's goods and sees his brother in need yet closes his heart against him, how does God's love abide in him?

I John 3:17

107 Let us not love in word or speech but in deed and in truth.

I John 3:18

108 And this commandment we have from him, that he who loves God should love his brother also.

I John 4:21

C. FROM OTHER SOURCES

109 Be thou loving and thankful to God for the least benefit that he giveth thee, and then thou shalt be the better prepared and more worthy to receive of him greater benefits.

The Imitation of Christ

110 You cannot all abandon your possessions, but at least you can change your attitude to them. At least you can see there is a taint in all getting. All getting separates you from other men; all giving unites you to them. Oh, believe me, all getting over and above your simplest needs, will be tainted with distress, and all giving will be a source of joy.

Attributed to St. Francis of Assisi, 1182–1226

111 Be charitable before wealth makes thee covetous, and lose not the glory of the mite. If riches increase, let thy mind hold peace with them.

Sir Thomas Browne, 1605–1682

112 Give all thou canst; high heaven rejects the lore of nicely-calculated less or more!

William Wordsworth, 1770–1850

113 Not what we give, but what we share,
　　　For the gift without the giver is bare;
　　　Who gives himself with his alms feeds three,
　　　Himself, his hungering neighbor, and me.

James Russell Lowell, 1819–1891

114 If thou hast abundance, give alms accordingly: if thou have but a little, be not afraid to give according to that little: for thou layest up a good treasure for thyself against the day of necessity.

Tobit 4:8–9

115   Christian Stewardship
is the dedication of all I am and have,
 under the control
of God's Spirit in Christ,
to the doing of his will,
in recognition of his lordship,
 in gratitude for his love,
 in every area of my life,
and in the serving of his redemptive fellowship.

The Life I Owe, William J. Keech

116 Lord, Thou didst suffer more for me
Than all the hosts of land and sea.
So let me render back again
This millionth of Thy gift. Amen.

Joyce Kilmer, 1886–1918

117 If the dignity of the giver be well considered, no gift
that he giveth shall seem little.

The Imitation of Christ

118 Give what you have. To someone it may be better
than you dare to think.

Henry Wadsworth Longfellow, 1807–1882

119 All things are Thine; no gift have we
Lord of all gifts, to offer Thee;
And hence with grateful hearts today
Thine own before Thy feet we lay.

John Greenleaf Whittier, 1807–1892

120 Did you breathe deeply of the fresh morning air?
Did you feel the warm noonday sun?
Did you smell sweet scent of wet autumn leaves?
These are God's gifts to you
Are your gifts to God in proportion?

121 From the heart bring forth incense of praise, from
the store of a good conscience bring forth the sacrifice of
faith, and whatsoever thou bringest forth kindle it with
love. These are the most acceptable offerings to God: mercy,
humility, confession, peace, love. It is thee that God seeketh
more than any gift.

St. Augustine, 354–430

122 Offer thyself unto God, and give thyself wholly for him; so shalt thine offering be accepted.

The Imitation of Christ

123 A poor man served by thee shall make thee rich;
A sick man helped by thee shall make thee strong;
Thou shalt be served thyself by every sense
Of service which thou renderest.

Elizabeth B. Browning, 1806–1861

124 I am only one—but still I am one;
I cannot do everything, but still I can do something.
And because I cannot do everything,
I will not refuse to do the something I can do.

Edward Everett Hale, 1822–1909

125 There is a destiny that makes us brothers,
None goes his way alone;
All that we send into the lives of others
Comes back into our own.

Edwin Markham, 1852–1940

126 It is not the work of one man that brings us to the goal.
It is the everlasting teamwork of every blooming soul.

Rudyard Kipling, 1865–1936

127 Grant us, Lord, the grace of giving
With a spirit large and free,
That ourselves and all our living
We may offer unto Thee.

Psalmodia Sacra, Gotha, 1715

128 The greatest grace of a gift, perhaps, is that it anticipates and admits of no return.

Henry Wadsworth Longfellow, 1807–1882

129 For we must share if we would keep
That blessing from above
Ceasing to give, we cease to have
Such is the law of love.

Richard C. Trench, 1807–1886

130   It is a good thing to fast, a better thing to fast and give to the poor.

St. Augustine, 354–430

131   My gracious Lord, I own Thy right
To every service I can pay
And call it my supreme delight
To hear Thy dictates and obey.

Philip Doddridge, 1702–1751

132   The test of generosity is not what we give, but what we have left.

Job Hodges

133   It is ours to offer what we can
His to supply what we cannot.

St. Jerome, 347–420

134   So live that when thy summons comes to give an account of thy stewardship, it may be done with joy, and not with grief.

135   Count your many blessings, name them one by one,
And it will surprise you what the Lord hath done.

J. Oatman, Jr.

136   There's nothing worth while but giving,
Giving of self and of love;
It's service that makes life worth living
A gift from the Master above.

137   This thing of giving, I do not understand, any more than you do, but there is something about it that blesses us. Those who give most have most left.

138   Give as you would if an angel
Awaited your gift at the door.
Give as you would if tomorrow
Found you where giving was o'er.

Give as you would to the Master
If you met His loving look
Give as you would of your substance
If His hand your offering took.

139   The heart that answers another's prayer is never empty. The more it gives, the more it gains.

140   Some give out of their abundance because they have understanding and a kind heart,
   Some give out of their own needs because they know the blessings of sacrifice,
   Some give without calculating because they love God,
   And all who give are rewarded in the measure of their giving.

141   Christian stewardship is the systematic and proportionate giving of time, abilities, and material possessions based on the conviction that these are a trust from God to be used in His service for the benefit of all mankind in grateful acknowledgment of Christ's redeeming love.

142   It should be said over and over that God has put enough provision into the hands of Christians to do everything in this world's work he expects the Church of Jesus Christ to do. Every mission could be financed, every hospital could be built, and every sanctuary could be provided, if God could count on a faithful stewardship among all people. Faithfulness is all he asks of any man.

Roy L. Smith

143   To give to my own church
   And by my gifts to help
   God's cause to triumph in a needy world,
   Is not to waste the bounty He has given
   But to invest it in the noblest way.

144   There are three kinds of giving: grudge-giving, duty-giving, and thanks-giving. Grudge-giving says, "I have to"; duty-giving says, "I ought to"; thanks-giving says, "I want to." The first comes from constraint, the second from a sense of obligation, the third from a full heart . . . Thanks-giving is an open gate into the love of God.

Thanks Be To God

145   I said it in the meadow path,
      I said it on the mountain stairs.
   The best things any mortal hath
      Are those which every mortal shares.

147

146 Give unto the Most High according as he hath enriched thee, and as thou hast gathered, give with a generous hand.

147 Learn the luxury of doing good.

Oliver Goldsmith, 1728–1774

148 Infinite is the help man can yield to man.

Thomas Carlyle, 1795–1881

149 Sacrificial power means to do the thing as God wants it done, no matter what we think or how we feel, and no matter what price we have to pay.

John R. Mott, 1865–1955

150 Giving is true having.

Charles Spurgeon, 1834–1892

151 We acknowledge that God has a total claim upon our whole life. We recognize his creative hand in the nature of life. We are grateful for his outpoured love in the experience of the redemptive power of Christ. Gladly yielding to the realities of this deep conviction, we bring to God our resources of personality, time, talent, and treasure as our offering to him and a fulfilling of the mission of the Church.

152 No great heart ever lacked compassion.

James Russell Lowell, 1819–1891

153 I shall pass through this world but once. If, therefore, there be any kindness I can show or any good thing I can do for any fellow creature, let me do it now; let me not defer it or neglect it, for I shall not pass this way again.

Étienne de Grellet, 1773–1855

154 The hand that gives, gathers.

Elizabeth Lloyd Howell, 1811–1896

155 Give me this day my daily bread
　　So I may share it with another,
　For in Your eyes, 'tis truly said,
　　All men are my brothers.

156   To give does not impoverish;
      To withhold does not enrich.

Joseph Addison, 1672–1719

157   Give freely to him that deserveth well and asketh nothing.

158   I gave, and giving,
      I grew richer . . .
      I comforted, and comforting,
        found peace.

159   It is hard to ask; it is sweet to give.

160   If any gift of mine may ease
      The burden of another
   God let me reach a loving hand,
      And be my brother's brother.

161   All for love, and nothing for reward.

Edmund Spenser, 1552–1599

162   The greatest object in the universe, says a certain philosopher, is a good man struggling with adversity; yet there is a still greater, which is the good man that comes to relieve it.

Oliver Goldsmith, 1728–1774

163   The best portion of a good man's life,
      His little nameless, unremembered acts
      Of kindness and of love.

William Wordsworth, 1770–1850

164   Charity is a virtue of the heart, and not of the hands.

Joseph Addison, 1672–1719

165   To give a little from a shiny store,
      Is that to give? To give and feel no loss,
      Is that to give as Christ gave on the Cross?

William F. Kirk, 1887–

166   In charity there is no excess, neither can angel or man come in danger by it.

Sir Francis Bacon, 1561–1626

167   It is good to have money and the things that money can buy, but it is good, too, to check up once in a while and make sure we haven't lost the things that money can't buy.
George Horace Lorimer, 1868–1937

168   We give Thee but Thine own,
Whate'er the gift may be:
All that we have is Thine alone,
A trust, O Lord, from Thee.
William Walsham Howe, 1823–1897

169   Man cannot live by bread alone. The making of money, the accumulation of material power, is not all there is to living. Life is something more than these, and the man who misses this truth misses the greatest joy and satisfaction that can come into his life—service for others.
Edward W. Bok, 1863–1930

170   To abound in wealth, to have fine houses and rich clothes, to be beautiful in our persons, to have titles of dignity, to be above our fellow-creatures, to overcome our enemies with power, to subdue all that oppose us, to set out ourselves in as much splendor as we can, to live highly and magnificently, to eat, and drink, and delight ourselves in the most costly manner, these are the great, the honorable, the desirable things, to which the spirit of the world turns the eyes of all people. But Jesus said, "What doth it profit a man if he gain the whole world and lose his own soul? What shall a man give in exchange for his life?"
William Law, 1686–1761

171   Eight degrees in giving:
>   He who gives grudgingly, reluctantly, or with regret;
>   He who gives less than he should, but gives graciously;
>   He who gives what he should, but only after he is asked;
>   He who gives before he is asked;
>   He who gives without knowing to whom he gives, although the recipient knows the identity of the donor;

He who gives without making his identity known;
He who gives without knowing to whom he gives,
neither does the recipient know from whom he
receives;
He who helps a fellow man to support himself.

Maimonides, 1135–1204

172 Father, bless the gifts we bring Thee,
Give them something good to do;
May they help someone to love Thee,
Father, may we love Thee too. Amen.

173 A man is rich in proportion to the things he can do
without . . . Sell your goods and keep your thoughts.

Henry David Thoreau, 1817–1862

174 Goodness is the only investment that never fails.

Henry David Thoreau, 1817–1862

175 May we Thy bounties thus
As stewards true receive,
And gladly, as Thou blessest us,
To Thee our first fruits give.

William Walsham Howe, 1823–1897

176 Solace other's troubles and your own disappear.

Joseph Addison, 1672–1719

177 God be praised for entrusting us with this holy
stewardship.
A world in need now summons us
To labor, love, and give;
To make our life an offering
To God, that men may live;
In gratitude and humble trust
We bring our best to thee
To serve thy cause and share thy love
With all humanity.

178 Teach us, good Lord, to serve thee as thou deservest;
to give and not to count the cost . . . To labor and not to
ask for reward, save in the knowledge that we do thy will.

St. Ignatius Loyola, 1491–1556

179 "Giving is living," the angel said,
    "Go feed to the hungry sweet charity's bread."
    "And must I keep giving and giving again?"
    My selfish and querulous answer ran—
    "Oh, no," said the angel, his eyes pierced me through,
    "Just give till the Master stops giving to you."

180 No one is so poor as to have nothing worth giving: as well might the mountain streamlets say they have nothing to give the sea because they are not rivers.

                    Henry Wadsworth Longfellow, 1807–1882

181 Back of the loaf is the snowy flour
    And back of the flour the mill,
    And back of the mill are the wheat and the shower
    And the sun and the Father's will.

                    Maltbie D. Babcock, 1858–1901

182 The most obvious lesson in Christ's teaching is that, there is no happiness in having and getting anything, but only in giving. I repeat, there is no happiness in having, or in getting, but only in giving.

                    William Henry Drummond, 1854–1907

183 A man there was,
    Some called him mad,
    The more he gave away,
    The more he had.

                    John Bunyan, 1628–1688

184 Into thy presence we bear our gifts,
    Each one a wise man of old:
        Incense the praise of grateful hearts
        Prayer more precious than gold;
        Myrrh is the gift that costs us most
        For it is our sorrow and pain,
    But we give it to Thee that thy Son
    May turn it to gladness again.

185 What I spent, I had;
    What I saved, I lost;
    What I gave, I have.

186   No man really gives unless the things he gives could
be of use to himself. The more useful it is and the more desirable, the greater becomes its value. He who gives such
things that he doesn't value or has no use for in reality gives
nothing.

Earl E. Marquiss

187   Who would have guessed?
    That our money is really another pair of feet to walk
        today where Christ would walk if he were still a
        man on earth?

    Or what is our money but another pair of hands to
        heal and feed and bless the desperate families of
        the earth?

    What is money but prayer of intercession suddenly
        crossing time and space to help answer its own in
        one swift unselfish gesture?

    What is money but our Other Self—either hard and
        cold and metallic like cash in a cash box—or warm
        and exciting and compassionate—tenderness in ac-
        tion.

    It is our Christian life!

188   We lose what on ourselves we spend,
    We have, as treasures without end,
    Whatever, Lord, to Thee we lend,
        Who givest all.

    Whatever, Lord, we lend to Thee,
    Repaid a thousandfold will be;
    Then gladly will we give to Thee,
        Who givest all!

Christopher Wordsworth, 1807–1885

189   You're asked to give not just what you can spare
    From your abundant store, but rather what
    You feel you ought to give, according as
    The Lord has blessed and prospered you.

190 You give but little when you give of your possessions.
It is when you give of yourself that you truly give.
For what are your possessions but things you keep
    and guard for fear you may need them tomorrow?
Kahlil Gibran, 1883–1931

191 The wise may bring their learning,
    The rich may bring their wealth,
And some may bring their greatness,
    And some bring strength and health;
We, too, would bring our treasures
    To offer to the King;
We have no wealth or learning:
    What shall we children bring?

We'll bring Him hearts that love Him;
    We'll bring Him thankful praise,
And young souls meekly striving
    To walk in holy ways:
And these shall be the treasures
    We offer to the King,
And these are gifts that even
    The poorest child may bring.

We'll bring the little duties
    We have to do each day;
We'll try our best to please Him,
    At home, at school, at play:
And better are these treasures
    To offer to our King,
Than richest gifts without them;
    Yet these a child may bring.
The Book of Praise for Children, 1881

192 Earthly goods are given to be used, not to be collected.
In the wilderness God gave Israel the manna every day, and
they had no need to worry about food and drink. Indeed, if
they kept any of the manna over until the next day, it went
bad. In the same way the disciple must receive his portion
from God every day. If he stores it up as a permanent pos-

session, he spoils not only the gift, but himself as well, for he sets his heart on his accumulated wealth, and makes it a barrier between himself and God. Where our treasure is, there is our trust, our security, our consolation and our God. Hoarding is idolatry.

Dietrich Bonhoeffer, 1906–1945

193 And there are those who give and know not pain in giving, nor do they seek joy, nor give with the mindfulness of virtue;
They give as in yonder valley the myrtle breathes its fragrance into space.
Through the hands of such as these God speaks, and from behind their eyes He smiles upon the earth.

Kahlil Gibran, 1883–1931

194 There are those who give little of the much which they have—and they give it for recognition and their hidden desire makes their gifts unwholesome.
And there are those who have little and give it all.
These are the believers in life and the bounty of life, and their coffer is never empty.
There are those who give with joy; and that joy is their reward.

Kahlil Gibran, 1883–1931

195 It is well to give when asked, but it is better to give unasked, through understanding;
And to the open-handed the search for one who shall receive is joy greater than giving.
And is there ought you would withhold?
All you have shall some day be given;
Therefore give now, that the season of giving may be yours and not your inheritors'.

Kahlil Gibran, 1883–1931

196 We praise Thee, O God, our Redeemer, Creator,
In grateful devotion our tribute we bring.
We lay it before Thee, we kneel and adore Thee.
We bless thy holy Name, glad praises we sing.

Julia Bulkley Cady Cory, 1902

197 I do not thank Thee, Lord,
That I have bread to eat while others starve;
Nor yet for work to do
While empty hands solicit Heaven;
Nor for a body strong
While other bodies flatten beds of pain.
No, not for these do I give thanks!

But I am grateful, Lord,
Because my meagre loaf I may divide;
For that my busy hands
May move to meet another's need;
Because my doubled strength
I may expend to steady one who faints.
Yes, for all these do I give thanks!

For heart to share, desire to bear
And will to lift,
Flamed into one by deathless Love—
Thanks be to God for this!
Unspeakable! His gift!

Janie Alford

198 Bring to God your gift, my brother; he'll not need
to call another—
You will do.
He will add his blessing to it; and the two of you
will do it—
God and you.

X

Offertory Prayers

1 Accept, O Lord, these offerings which Thy people make unto Thee, and grant that the cause to which they are devoted may prosper under Thy guidance to the glory of Thy name.

Devotional Services

2 O Lord, who didst commend the poor widow who gave her small gift which was her all into the treasury, bless all the gifts large or small that are offered when they are given in sacrifice and devotion. Make every gift do large service through thy grace. Accept the spirit of love and gratitude in our hearts, in Christ's name.

Book of Common Worship

3 O Lord our God, King of all the earth, accept of Thine infinite goodness the offerings of Thy people which, in honor of Thy name and with a free will and ready heart, they yield and dedicate unto Thee; and grant unto us Thy blessing, that the same being devoted to Thy service may be used for Thy glory and the welfare of Thy church.

Devotional Services

4 O Lord, who has taught us that all our doings without charity are nothing worth, and that it is more blessed to give than to receive, pour into the hearts of all thy people that most excellent gift of charity, and incline them to liberal offerings for the extension of thy Church and the salvation of mankind; and thus bringing forth the fruit of good works, may they by these be plenteously rewarded, and be made partakers of thy heavenly treasure; through the merits of Jesus Christ our most blessed Lord and Saviour.

Book of Common Worship

5 Keep us, O Lord, from spending wholly upon ourselves what we have received from Thee; and graciously accept our offerings this day, through Jesus Christ our Lord.

Devotional Services

6   O Lord Jesus, give us more charity, more self-denial, more likeness to Thee. Teach us to sacrifice our comforts for others' good. Make us kindly in thought, gentle in word, generous in deed. Teach us that it is better to give than to receive, better to forget ourselves than to seek our own, better to minister than to be ministered unto. And unto Thee, the Lord of love, be glory and praise forever.

Book of Common Worship

7   O God, who hast made us glad in the service of Thy house, may the blessing we have received not pass away from us. Accept our sacrifice of prayer and praise; and forgive the imperfection of our holy things; and when we go forth once more to our work in the world, do Thou, the God of labour and of rest, be with us throughout the week, and grant that even when our hands and our thoughts are occupied with daily toil our hearts may be at rest in Thee.

Devotional Services

8   Dear heavenly Father, help us to remember that the more we have given to us, the more we owe to Thee and to others. Help us to realize that the things we need to keep our bodies strong and develop our minds and spirits, are not given to us for our own selfish use, but in order that we may become more and more capable of doing things that will help to make the world better. May we make the most of every talent and opportunity thou hast given us. Show us how we can do this day by day.

Book of Common Worship

9   O God our Father, who didst give thine own Son for our life and salvation; give us such thankful hearts, we beseech thee, that our offering may be acceptable to thee.

A Book of Services and Prayers

10   Most gracious God, who hast called thy Church to worship thee; receive our sacrifice of praise; accept and bless this offering which we make; and give us grace to dedicate ourselves to thee; for the sake of Jesus Christ our Lord.

A Book of Services and Prayers

159

11   O Lord Jesus Christ, who for our sakes didst become poor, we pray thee to enlighten them that are rich in this world, that they may be not high-minded, nor trust in uncertain riches, but in thee, the living God, who givest us richly all things to enjoy. Grant them grace so to use their wealth that they may do good, and be rich in good works, ready to distribute and willing to communicate; laying up in store for themselves a good foundation against the time to come, that they may lay hold on eternal life.

Book of Common Worship

12   Receive, O Lord, we pray Thee, these our offerings which we render for the service of Thy church, and for the extension of Thy Kingdom, and accept with them our hearts and lives, which we desire to consecrate to Thee.

Pulpit and Parish Manual

13   Heavenly Father, giver of all good things, who hast taught us that it is more blessed to give than to receive; we dedicate these our offerings to the service of thy Church, humbly beseeching thee that all our gifts and energies may be consecrated to the extension of thy kingdom on earth.

A Book of Services and Prayers

14   Ever Blessed God, . . . we would bring to Thee the offering of glad and grateful hearts for Thy bounties to us, which are more than we can number. Help us ever to be mindful of Thy goodness and to show forth our love for Thee through our service to others.   *Minister's Service Book*

15   Almighty and most merciful Father, from whom cometh down every good and perfect gift, we give Thee hearty thanks for all Thy mercies; grant unto us with Thy gifts a heart to love Thee, and enable us to show our thankfulness for all Thy benefits by dedicating ourselves and all we have to Thy service.   *Euchologian, Book of Common Order, 1890*

16   Lord, that others may share what we so richly enjoy, we bring Thee now these gifts, praying that Thou wilt accept and use them to spread throughout the world the good news of Thy Son, our Saviour, Jesus Christ.

17　All things are Thine, O Lord, and of Thine own have we given Thee. We thank Thee for the abundance of Thy provision for our temporal needs, as well as for the deeper needs of the soul. And in gratitude we make these offerings, for the greater glory of him who, though he was rich, yet for our sakes became poor, that we through his poverty might become rich.　　　　　　　*Minister's Service Book*

18　O Lord, set the mark of thy cross upon the gifts that we have brought. May our offering be a true sacrifice and the glad expression of our love to thee. As thou sparest us till we fulfil thy purpose in this life, may our loving service abound yet more and more to the honor of thy great Name.
　　　　　　　A Book of Services and Prayers

19　O Thou who lovest a cheerful giver,
　　　　teach us by thy Spirit
　　　　to be thoughtful and prayerful in our giving.
　　Grant us the joy of the generous heart,
　　　　and the spirit of love and self-sacrifice
　　　　that was in Jesus Christ our Lord.
　　　　　　　R. W. Stewart

20　O Lord our God, send down upon us thy Holy Spirit, we beseech thee, to cleanse our hearts, to hallow our gifts, and to perfect the offerings of ourselves to thee, through Jesus Christ our Lord. Amen.
　　　　　　　Book of Common Order, Scotland

21　Eternal and Holy God; grant that we and thy whole church may ever rejoice in the fellowship of prayer and praise; in the fellowship of hearing thy gospel and making it known to others; and in the fellowship of giving and service.
　　　　　　　H. F. Leatherland

22　O Lord most bountiful; all things come of thee, and of thine own do we give thee. Now, therefore, our God, accept us thy servants and these offerings which we bring in devotion to thy most holy name, and give us grace evermore to serve thee with gladness of heart, through Jesus Christ our Lord. Amen.
　　　　　　　Book of Common Order, Scotland

161

23   O God our Father, as we bring this offering, we acknowledge our dependence upon thee; we thank thee for all
thy mercies; we pledge ourselves to be stewards of all that
thou hast entrusted to us; and we pray for all who are in
want of life's necessities.

H. F. Leatherland

24   Most gracious God, as we bring our gifts to thee, do
thou pardon and take away all our lukewarmness in thy
service.

Mercifully deal with us, not according to the poverty of
our devotion, but according to the riches of thy grace, in
Jesus Christ our Lord. Amen.

Book of Common Order, Scotland

25   Almighty God, our Heavenly Father, who hast spared
not thine only Son, but delivered him up for us all, and who
with him hast freely given us all things; help us, we beseech
thee, with all our gifts to yield ourselves to thee, that with
body, soul and spirit we may truly serve thee, and in thy
service find our deepest joy.

Service Book and Ordinal, South Africa

26   Almighty God, from whom cometh down every good
and perfect gift; accept, we beseech thee, the offerings of
thy people here present to thee with willing and thankful
hearts; and grant us so to consecrate ourselves to thy service
here that we may glorify thee hereafter in the heavenly
kingdom, through Jesus Christ our Lord. Amen.

Book of Common Order, Scotland

27   O God, who by thy Son didst teach us to see first the
kingdom and thy righteousness; grant us, as now in our
offering, so also in our daily life and work to glorify thee;
that, trusting in thy fatherly goodness, we may be set free
from anxiety and worldly care.

A Book of Services and Prayers

28   Lord of all Worlds, who art also our Father in heaven;
accept, we beseech thee, these offerings which we, thy children, make unto thee; and grant that the cause to which

they are devoted may prosper under thy guidance, to the good of the world, and advancement of thy kingdom, and the glory of thy name.

Service Book and Ordinal, South Africa

29   O Thou who dost seek in us that mind which was also in Christ Jesus, who humbled himself to become obedient unto death, even the death of the cross; grant us to be made after his likeness, that even these our gifts may be the symbols of a consecration that knows no bounds, and of a fellowship willingness to serve thee which holds nothing back; to thy praise and glory.

H. F. Leatherland

30   O God, most merciful and gracious, of whose bounty we have all received; accept, we beseech thee, this offering of thy people. Remember in thy love those who have brought it and those for whom it is given; and so follow it with thy blessing that it may promote peace and goodwill among men, and advance the kingdom of our Lord and Saviour, Jesus Christ.

Service Book and Ordinal, South Africa

31   O God, the source of all we venture in Thy sight to call our own; we invite Thee to look within our hearts and see that we make our offering in sincerity and with that tranquil conscience which is theirs who yield to Thee the degree and portion due of that material estate wherewith Thou has endowed them. And let that blessing come upon us which belongs to them of whom Thy servant spake from Thee saying: The Lord loveth a cheerful giver.

Let Us Worship God

32   Most Loving and Gracious God, our heavenly Father, do Thou, we entreat Thee, receive this our offering which we dedicate to Thee for the needs of Thy Church. It is of Thy bounty we are enabled to give this to Thee. And grant that now, and in all our giving, we may give joyfully with heartfelt gratitude, acknowledging in all things Thy fatherly goodness.

Let Us Worship God

33   O God, the Father of all Mercies, receive thou the offering which we bring thee at this time as a part of the worship of thy house. May these gifts be symbols of a consecration that knows no limit, that holds nothing back from thee who givest all; through Jesus Christ our Lord.

Service Book and Ordinal, South Africa

34   Our Father, we count it a privilege to be allowed to share in the task of bringing men to know and love Thee. Most gladly therefore do we bring our offering, praying Thy blessing upon it and upon those who have given it. May it be wisely used to the end that human hearts may be freed from ignorance, superstition and vice, and that Thy will may be done on earth as it is in heaven. In Jesus' Name we pray.

William S. Abernethy

35   All these good gifts have come to us from Thee. They were Thine to give and they are Thine also to curtail. They are not ours to keep; we do but hold them in truth; and only in continued dependence upon Thee, the Giver, can they be worthily enjoyed.

In that spirit accept them we pray.

John Baillie, 1886–1960 (adapted to plural)

36   Thanks be unto God for His unspeakable gift. To whom we bring our poor unworthy gifts, asking that they may be used for the advancement of the kingdom of our Lord and Saviour Jesus Christ in this and in all lands.

Let Us Worship God

37   O God, the Fountain of all good; we bring to Thee our gifts, according as Thou hast prospered us. Enable us, with our earthly things, to give Thee the love of our hearts and the service of our lives. Let Thy favor, which is life, and Thy loving-kindness, which is better than life, be upon us now and always, through Jesus Christ our Lord. Amen.

The Book of Common Order, Scotland

38   What shall we render unto the Lord for all his benefits towards us? Accept, O Lord, we beseech Thee, the gifts which Thy servants bring, and use them for Thine own high and holy ends, that Thy kingdom may be advanced and Thy will be done.

Let Us Worship God

offertory

Nikki Schindewolf

Ushers come forward to receive the offering
plates from Nikki. Nikki hands them to the
ushers.

OFFERTORY SENTENCE (Nikki Reads)

To give to the church
    And by my gifts to help
God's cause to triumph in a need world,
    Is not to waste the bounty he has given
But to invest it in the noblest way.

                    or

Give as you would if an angel
    Awaited your gift at the door
Give as you would if tomorrow
    Found you were giving was o'er
    Found you where giving was o'er

Give as you would to the Master
    If you met Hims loving look
Give as you would of your substance
    If His hand your offering took

When the offering plates arebrought forward,
let the ushers hold them while you say the prayer.

    Lord, that others may share what we so richly enj
enjoy, we bring you these gifts, praying that you
will accept them and use them to spread throughout
the world the good news of your son, our Savior,
Jesus Christ. Amen.

39   O Thou who in the days of Thy flesh didst sit over against the treasury of the temple, marking the gifts which the worshippers brought, and commending the spirit more than the gifts of the givers, be pleased to bless these offerings which with humble and grateful hearts Thy people lay at Thy feet.

Let Us Worship God

40   O Lord our God, who givest liberally and upbraidest not: teach us to give cheerfully of our substance for Thy cause and kingdom. Let Thy blessing be upon our offerings, and grant us to know the joy of those who give with their whole heart, through Jesus Christ our Lord. Amen.

The Book of Common Order, Scotland

41   We thank Thee, O heavenly Father, for the privilege of giving to Thee of that which Thou hast given to us. Help us to understand how to give, as becometh those who receive so richly of Thy bounty. May this offering be wisely spent, and carry a blessing with it. We ask it for Thy glory.

Evangelical Book of Worship

42   O Thou who hast taught us that a man is accepted of Thee according to that he hath, and not according to that he hath not, do Thou accept the gifts which Thy servants offer, and through Thy blessing upon them may they be used for the extension of Thy kingdom in this land and throughout the whole world. And forasmuch as the gift without the giver is bare, may we first of all offer ourselves willingly to Thy most blessed service, dedicating ourselves anew to Thee; and do Thou teach us, Lord, by our love to show something of how much we owe.

Let Us Worship God

43   O God, who needest not to be enriched with any gifts that we may bring, yet who lovest a cheerful giver: receive these our offerings which we present before Thee, and with them ourselves, our souls and our bodies, a living sacrifice, holy and acceptable to Thee, through Jesus Christ our Lord. Amen.

The Book of Common Order, Scotland

44   O Lord our God, in this that we offer Thee, we but give Thee what was always Thine. Accept our gift, together with the offering of our very selves; that while Thou blessest what we lay upon the Holy Table of our Lord, Christ Jesus, the benediction of Thy refreshing grace may descend upon Thy servants and renew us, with devoted and generous hearts, to love and serve Thee most faithfully in all our works and ways.

Let Us Worship God

45   All things are Thine; no gift have we
Lord of all gifts, to offer Thee.
And hence with grateful hearts today,
Thine own before Thy feet we lay.

46   All Gracious God, who of Thine infinite love didst give Thine only begotten Son, Jesus Christ, to die for our sins and rise again for our justification, and who hast made us partakers of the divine nature through the gift of the Holy Spirit; accept the offering which we now present to Thee; and grant that our bodies, souls and spirits may be unto Thee a living sacrifice, holy and well pleasing in Thy sight; and that, gaining faith in Thy strength, we may be able truly to serve Thee, and in all things to obey Thy will.

Evangelical Book of Worship

47   Almighty and Ever-blessed God, who in the abundance of Thy goodness dost ever give us more than we desire or dare to ask: pour forth upon us, we beseech Thee, a spirit of thankfulness and increase in us that most blessed grace of charity, that we may ever be more willing to give than to receive; and so rule our hearts that all we have may be used for Thy service, and we ourselves be consecrated to Thee, through Jesus Christ our Lord. Amen.

Book of Common Order, Scotland

48   O God, who openest Thine hand and satisfieth the desire of every living creature, receive, we pray Thee, this offering of Thy people, the symbol of their love and the pledge

of their devotion. Remember graciously all who have given and so speed and prosper their gifts that Thy kingdom may come, and Thy will be done on earth as it is in heaven.

Arthur W. Cleaves, in *Minister's Service Book*

49   Our Father, we humbly beseech Thee, to accept our offerings this day. May they accomplish much good by Thy blessing. We ask it in Jesus' name.

Evangelical Book of Worship

50   Almighty God, our Father, by whose will we came into being, and by whose grace we are sustained: with grateful hearts we acknowledge Thy power and Thy love. In token of our appreciation of all Thou hast done for us, we bring these gifts today, praying that Thou wilt bless and use both them and us in the service of Thy kingdom.

James Dalton Morrison

51   O God, our Father, be pleased to accept this offering of our money, the symbol of our love and devotion; and give Thy servants grace so to use it that Thy name may be honored among men, and the happiness and prosperity of Thy church increased.

Arthur W. Cleaves, in *Minister's Service Book*

52   Heavenly Father, we present our offerings to Thee in Thy house, the place where Thine honor dwelleth. We realize these gifts are in no sense whatever an equivalent for what Thou hast done for us. But be graciously pleased to accept these our temporal gifts, and help us, that in the struggle for worldly comforts, we may not forget to lay up treasures in heaven. We ask it in Jesus' name.

Evangelical Book of Worship

53   Enable us, O God, to glorify thee with our offerings, that the life of the world may be enriched with the overflow of goodness from the cup of blessing which thou hast filled so bountifully.

Minister's Book of Prayers

54   Almighty God, whose loving hand hath given us all that we possess, grant us grace that we may honor thee with our substance, and, remembering the account which we must one day give, may we be faithful stewards of thy bounty.

Book of Common Prayer

55   O God who dost teach us by this act of worship that it is more blessed to give than to receive, graciously accept these our offerings and give us the right spirit both in giving and receiving.

56   O Thou God of all blessings, we pray Thee to accept what we offer Thee with grateful hearts. May we learn to give cheerfully at all times, since Thou, Lord, lovest a cheerful giver. May our offering be blessed, as it is sent forth in Thy Name. May we, as a people go on from glory to glory, till we come into the unity of the faith, and of the knowledge of the Son of God, unto a perfect man, unto the measure of the stature of the fullness of Christ. We ask it in Jesus' name.

Evangelical Book of Worship

57   Accept these offerings now placed upon thine altar, O God, giver of every good and perfect gift. Grant that they may be symbols of our love and of ourselves, now offered more fully to thee. Use these gifts and us, we beseech thee, to the end that thy kingdom may come and thy will be done on earth even as it is done in heaven.

A Book of Worship for Free Churches

58   Receive, O Lord, we pray Thee, these offerings which we render for the service of Thy church, and for the extension of Thy kingdom, and accept them with our hearts and lives, which we desire to consecrate to Thee.

Pulpit and Parish Manual

59   Grant, O Lord, to thy people, when they offer of their substance to thee in this place, that they may feel and know that it is more blessed to give than to receive, and that with such sacrifices thou art well pleased; and that their alms may come up as a memorial before Thee.

Book of Common Prayer, Canada

60   Almighty God, our heavenly Father, prosper every good work undertaken by Thy church according to Thy will and give unto all of us Thy servants the spirit of him who came not to be ministered unto but to minister, and whose joy it was to do Thy will in helping men.

Book of Church Services

61   Giver of Every Good and Perfect Gift, all the gold and silver are thine, and the cattle on a thousand hills are thine, and the world is thine, and we are thine. Accept this portion of the fruit of our toil, we beseech thee, together with our labor and love; and grant us grace to consecrate not only our silver but ourselves to thy service, according to the measure and pattern of Him who gave Himself for us.

The Pilgrim Hymnal

62   O God, the giver of every good and perfect gift, give us skill and imagination to use the gifts which we now place on Thy holy table. May this money be used by dedicated hands to further Thy Kingdom, to create fellowship, and to bring the healing power of the gospel into the lives of men; through Jesus Christ our Lord.

Acts of Worship

63   We could give Thee nothing, O Thou great Giver of every good and perfect gift, if Thou hadst not first given it to us. Grant us grace to so please ourselves with what seems for the moment to be ours that we shall in deed and in truth please Thee with what is eternally Thine.

The Pilgrim Hymnal

64   O our Lord, we offer thee all that is good in us, though it be very small and imperfect, in order that thou mayest award and sanctify it, that thou mayest make it acceptable to thee, and always be perfecting it more and more.

Thomas à Kempis, *ca.* 1441

65   O God, bless, if thou canst, the ways in which we have earned this money, and accept our thanks for all honorable means of earning a living. Help us to see work that is its own reward, in which we grow in inward grace and strength and in the doing of which we find fellowship with others.

Acts of Worship

66   O Lord Jesus, who has taught us that to whomsoever much is given, of him shall much be required; grant that we, whose lot is cast in this Christian heritage, may strive more earnestly, by our prayers and tithes, by sympathy and study, to hasten the coming of Thy kingdom among all people of the earth, that as we have entered into the labors of others, so others may enter into ours, to Thy honor and glory.

A. S. T. Fisher

67   Heavenly Father, who hast given us all things richly to enjoy; graciously deign to receive these our gifts which we now lay upon thine altar, and bless us both in the use and the giving of thy mercies; for Jesus' sake.

Pulpit and Parish Manual

68   Lord God, we thank thee for the privilege of giving, without which our lives would be impoverished indeed. We pray for grace to give well, to help without patronizing, to assist without weakening, to share without diminishing the self-respect of others.

Acts of Worship

69   Be pleased, O God, to bless what we offer, to approve it fully, to make it spiritual and well-pleasing to you.

Feast of St. Bartholomew, Roman Missal

70   Accept, O Lord, these gifts of our substance and grant that they may be used for the extension of thy kingdom and the greater glory of thy holy name.

Elmore McNeill McKee

71   Almighty God, who didst so love the world as to give thine only begotten Son; mercifully grant that these our gifts may be found before thee as a worthy token of our love; and inasmuch as all that we both have and are is thine, teach us, we earnestly beseech thee, in all our offerings humbly and gratefully to bring unto thee the offering of ourselves.

H. Bisseker

72   Father, bless the gifts we bring to Thee,
Give them something good to do;
May they help someone to love Thee,
Father, may we love Thee, too.

73   A part of ourselves we give, O God;
     A part of ourselves we consecrate here.
    Claim our whole selves, O God,
      Time, talents, all,
    Till our surrendered lives,
      Thy plans fulfill.

Betty Jane and J. Martin Bailey

74   Our Father, since thou dost freely give us all things, help us to give ourselves to thee with these gifts which are only the symbols of our devotion.

James E. Wagner

75   We give thee, Lord, what is thine own, for all we have comes of thy bounty to enrich our lives. Grant us grace with these outward offerings to present ourselves willingly before thee, dedicated anew to thy service in the spirit of Jesus Christ.

76   Almighty God, giver of every good and perfect gift; help us rightly to render to thee all that we have and all that we are, that we may praise thee not with our lips, but with our whole lives turning the duties, the sorrows, and the joys of all our days into a living sacrifice to thee.

77   We humbly ask and beg you, most kind and gracious Father, through Jesus Christ, your Son, our Lord, to receive and bless these gifts which we offer to you for your Church.

Feast of St. Bartholomew, Roman Missal

78   Father of mankind, accept the gifts we place on thine altar for the service they can render and as tokens of our renewed dedication to thy kingdom of love for all men.

Christian Worship: A Service Book

79   Heart and mind, possessions, Lord, I offer unto thee;
    All these were mine, Lord; thou didst give them all
      to me.
    Wondrous are thy doings unto me. Plans and my
      thoughts and everything
    I ever do are dependent on thy will and love alone.
    I commit my spirit unto thee.
    Heart and mind, possessions, Lord, I offer unto thee;
    Thou art the Way, the Truth; thou art the life.

Narayan V. Tilak, India, 1862–1909

80   We thank thee, O God, and offer thee the first fruits which thou hast given us. Thou produced them by means of thy word, commanding the earth, to bring forth every kind of fruit for the joy and nutriment of all men and beasts.

We praise thee, O Lord, for thy gifts, for giving us the entire creation of many fruits through thy Son, Jesus Christ, our Saviour.

Through Him shalt thou be held glorious for endless centuries. Amen!

Benediction of the First Fruits

81   Almighty God, who from ancient times hast put it into the hearts of Thy people to make offerings for Thy service and use of Thy house, and who hast been pleased at all times to accept gifts at their hands, we hereby dedicate to Thee and Thy church these gifts of Thy people. May Thy blessing rest upon them that Thy kingdom may be advanced and Thy name exalted in all the world, and that all men everywhere may seek after Thee and find Thee.

St. James Church, New York

82   Grant us, Lord, the grace of giving
With a spirit large and free,
That ourselves and all our living
We may offer unto Thee.

Psalmodia Sacra, Gotha, 1715

83   Not what we give, but what we share,
For the gift without the giver is bare;
Who gives himself with his alms feeds three—
Himself, his hungering neighbor, and Me.

James Russell Lowell, 1819–1891

84   Spirit of Truth, of Life, of Pow'r
We bring ourselves as gifts to Thee;
Oh, bind our hearts this sacred hour
In faith and hope and charity.

Horace Westwood, 1884–

85   Bless thou the gifts our hands have brought;
Bless thou the work our hearts have planned;
Ours is the faith, the will, the thought;
The rest, O God, is in thy hand.

Samuel Longfellow, 1819–1892

86 Help us, O God, to maintain within ourselves a constant spirit of gratitude toward Thee, to remember that not in words and songs alone should we express our thankfulness; our deeds should speak thy praise; our willingness to share with others should testify to our gratitude.

Union Prayer Book

87 In gratitude and humble trust
We bring our best to thee
To serve thy cause and share thy love
With all humility.

88 With hearts that are grateful for all the good things that are ours, we bring our gifts to Thee.

89 May we add to these gifts the more precious offering of vigorous lives, dedicated to the service of mankind.

90 We bring these offerings, Our Father, in the spirit of Jesus who taught us to share with one another the blessings which come to us from Thee.

91 O God, we dedicate this offering to thy service and we present ourselves here that we may work with Thee in making beautiful the world of men.

92 O God, who art known to us as a Spirit, and Light, and Power, and Love; we offer thee now, together with these gifts, our lives to be used in thy service.

93 Lord of all worlds, who art also our Father in heaven, accept, we beseech Thee, these offerings which we thy children make unto Thee, and grant that the cause to which they are devoted may prosper under thy guidance, to the good of the world, the advancement of thy kingdom, and the glory of thy name, through Jesus Christ our Lord.

Service Book and Ordinal, South Africa

94 In grateful remembrance of all the good gifts that we have received, we bring this offering.

95 Our Father, great shepherd of us all, accept this our offering, we pray. As it comes from our thankful hearts, so transform it that it may bless multitudes whom not having seen, we love.

96   In the spirit of this season of goodwill we bring these gifts. And we offer ourselves that through us goodwill may be increased on earth.

97   Our Father, since thou dost freely give us all things, help us to give ourselves to thee with these gifts which are but symbols of our devotion.

98   We offer these our gifts to Thee, O Lord, believing that as they are dedicated to Thy service their usefulness may be multiplied. Accept them in that spirit we pray.

99   Unto Thee, O giver of the true gift, we bring our offering for blessing. Unite us by these portions of our lives with those who will benefit from them. Take away all pride, all condescension, all sentimentality, but leave our Love, O Father of Jesus. For unto Thee be all glory and majesty, even unto earth's end.

100   Dear Heavenly Father, as thou didst increase the five loaves and two fishes, the gift of a child, to feed the multitude, so transform this our offering, given out of thankful hearts, that it may bless multitudes, whom having not seen, we love.

101   May the gifts we bring
Be used in our Church,
O God,
To tell the people of (name your town)
And others far away,
About your love for us all.

102   Thanks be to Thee, O God, for opening our minds and our hearts to the material and spiritual needs of Thy kingdom and for putting strength in our arms so that we could labor profitably and produce of our bounty sufficient to offer Thee these gifts.

103   O God, from whom we receive both our gifts and our power to give: grant that these offerings which we bring to thee may be used for thy glory.

A Book of Services and Prayers

104   Unto Thee, O giver of every good and perfect gift, we bring our offering for blessing. Unite us by these portions of our lives with those who will benefit from them.

105   With hearts that are grateful for all the good things that are ours, we bring our gifts to Thee.

106   O God, who didst so love the world as to give Thine only Son for its redemption, help us to love Thee as Thou didst first love us, and give—time, talent, possessions, and with them all ourselves.

James E. Wagner

107   Holy Father, who, through the blood of thy dear Son, has consecrated for us a new and living way to thy throne of grace, we come to thee through Him, unworthy as we are, and we humbly beseech thee to accept and use us and these our gifts for thy glory. All that is in heaven and earth is thine, and of thine own do we give to thee.

Book of Common Worship, South India

108   Almighty God, we humbly beseech thee, to accept the offerings which we have presented unto thee, and mercifully to receive our supplications and prayers; and grant that those things which we have faithfully asked according to thy will, may effectually be obtained, to the relief of our necessity and to the setting forth of thy glory.

The Book of Common Prayer, Ireland

109   With these gifts we bring Thee, Our Father, our grateful thanks for all thy goodness to us. Receive them, we pray Thee, and us.

110   With grateful hearts we bring our gifts to Thee, O God, for we are reminded anew of Thy great goodness to us. Help us ever to remember that the gift for which Thy Father-heart most fondly yearns is not the gift of our silver and our gold, but the gift of our own selves, in glad and loving surrender to Thee.

James Dalton Morrison

111   Minister: To the preaching of the good tidings of salvation

        People: We consecrate our gifts

        Minister: To the teaching of Jesus' way of life

        People: We consecrate our gifts

        Minister: To the healing of broken bodies and the soothing of fevered brows

        People: We consecrate our gifts

        Minister: To the leading of every little child to the knowledge and love of Jesus

        People: We consecrate our gifts

        Minister: To the caring of helpless age and relief of all who look to us for help

        People: We consecrate our gifts

        Minister: To the evangelization of the world and the building of the kingdom of God.

        People: We consecrate our gifts, our efforts and our lives.

Book of Common Worship

112   Unto Thee, O Lord, do we offer the gift of our hands and the loyalty of our hearts. Accept us with our gifts, we pray, in Jesus' Name.

W. Earl Ledden

XI

Sentences
and
Prayers
Before
the Sermon

1   Let the words of my mouth and the meditation of my
      heart be acceptable in thy sight,
   O Lord, my rock and my redeemer.

Psalms 19:14

2   Now to him who by the power at work within us is
able to do far more abundantly than all that we ask or think,
to him be glory in the church and in Christ Jesus to all
generations, for ever and ever. Amen.

Ephesians 3:20–21

3   O God, forasmuch as without thee we are not able to
please thee; mercifully grant that thy Holy Spirit may in all
things direct and rule our hearts; through Jesus Christ our
Lord. Amen.

Gelasian Sacramentary, 6th century

4   O God, Author of eternal light, do thou shed forth continual day upon us who watch for thee; that our lips may
praise thee, our life may bless thee, our meditations may
glorify thee, through Jesus Christ our Lord. Amen.

Sarum Breviary, 12th century

5   O Lord, from whom all good things do come, grant to
us thy humble servants, that by thy holy inspiration we may
think those things that are good, and by thy merciful guiding may perform the same.

Book of Common Prayer

6   O Thou, without whom nothing is strong and nothing
is holy, may our speaking and hearing at this time be to the
quickening and increase of our faith and hope and love, and
to the glory of Thy Name.

Devotional Services

7   O Lord God, who hast left unto us thy holy word to be
a lamp unto our feet and a light unto our path; give unto us
all thy Holy Spirit, we humbly pray thee, that out of the
same word we may learn what is thy blessed will, and frame
our lives in all holy obedience to the same, to thine honor
and glory and the increase of our faith; through Jesus Christ
our Lord.

A Book of Public Worship

8   O God, by whom the meek are guided in judgment and light riseth up in darkness for the godly; grant us, in our doubts and uncertainties, the grace to ask what thou wouldst have us to do, that the spirit of wisdom may save us from false choices, and that in thy light we may see light, and in thy straight path may not stumble.

Ancient Collects

9   O God, who hast taught us that man doth not live by bread alone, but by every word that proceedeth out of thy mouth; grant us ever to hunger after the heavenly food of thy word, which thou hast given for our nourishment unto eternal life; through Jesus Christ our Lord.

A Book of Worship for Free Churches

10   Almighty God, in whom are hid all the treasures of wisdom and knowledge; open our eyes that we may behold wondrous things out of thy law; and give us grace that we may clearly understand and heartily choose the way of thy commandments, through Jesus Christ our Lord. Amen.

Book of Common Order, Scotland

11   Blessed Lord, who hast caused all sacred Scriptures to be written for our learning; we thank Thee for the signs of Thy providence and inspiration in many lands; and we desire of Thee the gifts of insight and wisdom, or patience and charity, so to read the letter of things written in olden times, that Thy Holy Spirit of truth may ever live in us; and that we may so meditate on the story of things temporal, as ever to worship Thee the Living and Eternal God.

Devotional Services

12   Merciful Father, who willest not Thy children should wander in darkness; pour the light of Thy Spirit into our minds and hearts, that we may discover what is Thy holy will, and discern the true from the false, the evil from the good, that we may henceforth walk in all humility in the paths of heavenly wisdom and peace, to the glory of Thy holy Name.

Devotional Services

13   Almighty God, grant us, we beseech thee, so to speak, so to hear, and so to learn that our fears may be banished, our minds enlightened, our hearts kindled, our faith increased, and our steps directed unto thee.

The Pilgrim Hymnal

14   O Lord our God, who hast given thy word to be a lamp unto our feet and a light unto our path; grant us grace to receive thy truth in faith and love, that by it we may be prepared unto every good word and work, to the glory of thy Name, through Jesus Christ our Lord. Amen.

The Book of Common Order, Scotland

15   O invisible God, who seest all things, yet whom none can see; Father of lights, whom to know is eternal life, yet whom none can know unless Thou dost show him Thy glory; vouchsafe of Thine infinite mercy, now and ever, to enlighten our minds and hearts to know Thee and Thy holy and perfect will. Let us not follow after shadows, but bring our feet into the way of truth; and may we ever continue to abide therein, following all the days of our life in the steps of Jesus Christ our Lord.

Devotional Services

16   Almighty God, from whom every good prayer cometh, and who pourest out on all who desire it the spirit of grace and supplication; deliver us, when we draw nigh to thee, from coldness of heart and wanderings of mind, that with steadfast thoughts and kindled affections we may worship thee in spirit and in truth.

Ancient Collects

XII

Sentences
and
Prayers
After
the Sermon

1   For this reason I bow my knees before the Father, from whom every family in heaven and on earth is named, that according to the riches of his glory he may grant you to be strengthened with might through his Spirit in the inner man, and that Christ may dwell in your hearts through faith; that you, being rooted and grounded in love, may have power to comprehend with all the saints what is the breadth and length and height and depth, and to know the love of Christ which surpasses knowledge that you may be filled with all the fulness of God.

Ephesians 3:14–19

2   Now to him who by the power at work within us is able to do far more abundantly than all that we ask or think, to him be glory in the church and in Christ Jesus to all generations, for ever and ever. Amen.

Ephesians 3:20–21

3   To the King of ages, immortal, invisible, the only God, be honor and glory for ever and ever. Amen.

I Timothy 1:17

4   (To him) who alone has immortality and dwells in unapproachable light, whom no man has ever seen or can see. To him be honor and eternal dominion. Amen.

I Timothy 6:16

5   The God of all grace, who has called you to his eternal glory in Christ, will himself restore, establish, and strengthen you. To him be the dominion for ever and ever. Amen.

I Peter 5:10–11

6   Now to him who is able to keep you from falling and to present you without blemish before the presence of his glory with rejoicing, to the only God, our Saviour through Jesus Christ our Lord be glory, majesty, dominion, and authority, before all time and now and for ever. Amen.

Jude 24–25

7   Follow with thy blessing, O Lord, the preaching of Thy Holy Word; take it home to our hearts and consciences;

and help us ever in Thy faith and fear: through Jesus Christ our Lord.

Let Us Worship God

8   And now unto God our Father, we would, as is most meet, with the Church on earth and the Church in heaven, ascribe all honour and glory, as it was in the beginning, is now, and ever shall be, world without end.

9   Almighty God, we invoke Thee, the Fountain of everlasting light; and entreat thee to send forth thy truth into our hearts, and to pour upon us the glory of thy brightness.

Sarum Breviary, 12th Century

10   Almighty God, who hast given us grace at this time with one accord to make our common supplications unto thee; and dost promise that when two or three are gathered together in thy name thou wilt grant their requests; fulfil now, O Lord, the desires and petitions of thy servants, as may be most expedient for them; granting us in this world knowledge of thy truth, and in the world to come life everlasting.

St. John Chrysostom, 345–407

11   Suffer not, O God, the good seed, which the Son of man hath sown, to be caught away by the wicked one out of our hearts, or to be scorched by tribulation or persecution, or to be choked with cares and pleasures of this life; but being received into good and honest hearts, may it bring forth in us abundantly the fruits of faith and obedience; through our Lord and Saviour Jesus Christ.

Book of Common Order, 1896

12   Grant, we beseech thee, Almighty God, that the words which we have heard this day with our outward ears may, through thy grace, be so grafted in our hearts that they may bring forth in us the fruit of good living, to the honor and praise of thy Name.

Book of Common Prayer

13   Grant, Lord, that what we have said with our lips, we may believe in our hearts and practice in our lives; and of thy mercy keep us faithful; through Jesus Christ our Lord.

A Book of Worship

14   Let Thy Gospel, O Lord, come unto us not in word only but in power, and in much assurance, and in the Holy Ghost, that we may be guided into all truth, and strengthened unto all obedience and enduring of Thy will with joyfulness; that, abounding in the work of faith, and the labour of love, and the patience of hope, we may finally be made partakers of the inheritance of the saints in light.

Book of Common Order, 1896

15   O God, who hast sounded in our ears Thy divine and saving oracles; enlighten our souls to the full understanding of what has been spoken, that we may not only be hearers of spiritual words, but also doers of good works; following after faith, unfeigned, blameless life, and conversation without reproach.

Litany of St. James, 1st Century

16   O God, who didst teach the hearts of Thy faithful people, by sending them the light of Thy Holy Spirit, grant us, by the same Spirit, to have a right understanding of Thy saving Truth. Visit, we pray Thee, this congregation with Thy love and favour; and enlighten our minds more and more with the light of the everlasting Gospel.

Book of Common Order, 1896

17   Almighty God, grant unto thy people that they may love the things which thou commandest, and desire that which thou dost promise; that so, among the sundry and manifold changes of the world, our hearts may surely there be fixed, where true joys are to be found.

The Pilgrim Hymnal

18   Father of mercies, and God of all comfort, we joyfully acknowledge Thine infinite goodness in sending to us the day-spring from on high to enlighten our darkness, and guide our feet into the way of peace. We praise Thy name for those portions of Thy holy Word of which Thou hast made us partakers this day. Grant that they may bring forth fruit unto holiness in our whole life, to the glory of Thy name, the edification of our brethren, and the comfort of our souls in the day of our Lord Jesus Christ.

Book of Common Order, 1896

19   O Lord, God of our life, who hast given us the rest of sacred day, grant that the benediction of its restfulness may

abide upon us throughout the week. Enable us to carry the influence of its consecration into all that we do; let the praises of our lips rendered to thee this day become praise in our lives. May the power of love be with us in every duty; that by pureness, by knowledge, by tenderness we may glorify thee.   W. Boyd Carpenter, 19th Century

20   O God, our true and highest life, by whom, through whom, and in whom all things live, which live truly and blessedly; we humbly pray thee so to guide and govern us by thy Holy Spirit, that in all the cares and occupations of our daily life we may never forget thee, but remember that we are ever walking in thy sight.

Service Book and Ordinal, South Africa

21   Grant, O Lord, that what we have sung with our lips we may believe in our hearts; and what we believe in our hearts, we may practice in our lives; so that being doers of the word and not hearers only, we may obtain life.

Book of Common Worship

22   Eternal God, the Source of all wisdom, who willest not that thy children should wander in darkness, pour the light of thy spirit into our minds and hearts that, discovering what is thy holy will, we may discern the true from the false, the evil from the good, and may henceforth walk in the paths of wisdom and of good will.

Henry Hallam Tweedy, 1868–1953

23   Sanctify, O Lord, both our coming in and our going forth; and grant that when we leave thy house, we may not leave thy presence. So shall we practice in our lives what we have said with our lips and believed in our hearts, and bring forth the fruit of good living.

24   We thank Thee, O Lord, that we have been permitted to hear and meditate on Thy holy Word; and we beseech Thee that its lessons may be fixed in our memories, and impressed upon our hearts and that they may bring forth in our lives the peaceable fruits of righteousness to the glory of Thy holy Name.

Book of Common Order, 1896

25   O God . . . enlighten our souls by the preaching of Thy truth, and, at this time, bless unto us whatever has been spoken in accordance with Thy mind and purpose. And grant that we may be not only hearers of spiritual words, but also doers of good works, and that in the world we may walk by faith, show forth a blameless life, irreproachable before Thee and in the sight of all.

Let Us Worship God

XIII

Scripture
Verses
for Communion

1 Man shall not live by bread alone, but by every word that proceeds from the mouth of God.

Matthew 4:4

2 Seeing the crowds, he went up on the mountain, and when he sat down his disciples came to him. And he opened his mouth and taught them, saying:

> Blessed are the poor in spirit, for theirs is the kingdom of heaven.
> Blessed are those who mourn, for they shall be comforted.
> Blessed are the meek, for they shall inherit the earth.
> Blessed are those who hunger and thirst for righteousness, for they shall be satisfied.
> Blessed are the merciful, for they shall obtain mercy.
> Blessed are the pure in heart, for they shall see God.
> Blessed are the peacemakers, for they shall be called sons of God.
> Blessed are those who are persecuted for righteousness' sake, for theirs is the kingdom of heaven.
> Blessed are you when men revile you and persecute you and utter all kinds of evil against you falsely on my account.
> Rejoice and be glad, for your reward is great in heaven, for so men persecuted the prophets who were before you.

Matthew 5:1–12

3 Let your light so shine before men, that they may see your good works and give glory to your Father who is in heaven.

Matthew 5:16

4 Whoever then relaxes one of the least of these commandments and teaches men so, shall be called least in the kingdom of heaven; but he who does them and teaches them shall be called great in the kingdom of heaven.

Matthew 5:19

5 So if you are offering your gift at the altar, and there remember that your brother has something against you, leave your gift there before the altar and go; first be reconciled to your brother, and then come and offer your gift.

Matthew 5:23–24

6   You have heard that it was said, "You shall love your neighbor and hate your enemy." But I say to you, Love your enemies and pray for those who persecute you, so that you may be sons of your Father who is in heaven.

Matthew 5:43–45

7   And if you salute only your brethren, what more are you doing than others? Do not even the Gentiles the same?

Matthew 5:47

8   You, therefore, must be perfect, as your heavenly Father is perfect.

Matthew 5:48

9   For if you forgive men their trespasses, your heavenly Father also will forgive you.

Matthew 6:14

10   Do not lay up for yourselves treasures on earth, where moth and rust consume and where thieves break in and steal, but lay up for yourselves treasures in heaven, where neither moth nor rust consumes and where thieves do not break in and steal. For where your treasure is there will your heart be also.

Matthew 6:19–21

11   No one can serve two masters; for either he will hate the one and love the other, or he will be devoted to the one and despise the other. You cannot serve God and mammon.

Matthew 6:24

12   But seek first his kingdom and his righteousness, and all these things shall be yours as well.

Matthew 6:33

13   Ask, and it will be given you; seek, and you will find; knock, and it will be opened to you. For every one who asks receives, and he who seeks finds, and to him who knocks it will be opened.

Matthew 7:7–8

14   So whatever you wish that men would do to you, do so to them; for this is the law and the prophets.

Matthew 7:12

15　Not every one who says to me, "Lord, Lord," shall enter the kingdom of heaven, but he who does the will of my Father who is in heaven.

Matthew 7:21

16　Every one then who hears these words of mine and does them will be like a wise man who built his house upon the rock; and the rain fell, and the floods came, and the winds blew and beat upon that house, but it did not fall, because it had been founded on the rock.

Matthew 7:24–25

17　Then he said to his disciples, "The harvest is plentiful, but the laborers are few."

Matthew 9:37

18　But I tell you, it shall be more tolerable on the day of judgment for Tyre and Sidon than for you.

Matthew 11:22

19　Come to me, all who labor and are heavy-laden, and I will give you rest. Take my yoke upon you, and learn from me; for I am gentle and lowly in heart, and you will find rest for your souls. For my yoke is easy, and my burden is light.

Matthew 11:28–30

20　If any man would come after me, let him deny himself and take up his cross and follow me.

Matthew 16:24

21　Truly, I say to you unless you turn and become like children, you will never enter the kingdom of heaven.

Matthew 18:3

22　Let the children come to me, and do not hinder them; for to such belongs the kingdom of heaven.

Matthew 19:14

23　Whoever would be great among you must be your servant and whoever would be first among you must be your slave; even as the Son of man came not to be served but to serve, and to give his life as a ransom for many.

Matthew 20:26–28

24   You shall love the Lord your God with all your heart, and with all your soul, and with all your mind. This is the great and first commandment. And a second is like it, you shall love your neighbor as yourself.

Matthew 22:37–39

25   All authority in heaven and on earth has been given to me. Go therefore and make disciples of all nations, baptizing them in the name of the Father and of the Son and of the Holy Spirit; and lo, I am with you always.

Matthew 28:18–20

26   Truly, I say to you, there is no one who has left house or brothers or sisters or mother or father or children or lands, for my sake and for the gospel, who will not receive a hundredfold now in this time.

Mark 10:29–30

27   If any man would come after me, let him deny himself and take up his cross daily and follow me. For whoever would save his life will lose it; and whoever loses his life for my sake, he will save it.

Luke 9:23–24

28   Blessed rather are those who hear the word of God and keep it!

Luke 11:28

29   Every one to whom much is given, of him will much be required; and of him to whom men commit much they will demand the more.

Luke 12:48

30   Behold, Lord, the half of my goods I give to the poor; and if I have defrauded any one of anything, I restore it fourfold.

Luke 19:8

31   For God so loved the world that he gave his only Son, that whoever believes in him should not perish but have eternal life.

John 3:16

191

32   He who believes in him is not condemned; he who does not believe is condemned already, because he has not believed in the name of the only Son of God.

John 3:18

33   Whoever drinks of the water that I shall give him will never thirst; the water that I shall give him will become in him a spring of water welling up to eternal life.

John 4:14

34   Truly, truly I say to you, he who hears my word and believes him who sent me, has eternal life; he does not come into judgment, but has passed from death to life.

John 5:24

35   Truly, truly, I say to you, it was not Moses who gave you the bread from heaven; my Father gives you the true bread from heaven.

John 6:32

36   I am the bread of life; he who comes to me shall not hunger, and he who believes in me shall never thirst.

John 6:35

37   I am the light of the world; he who follows me will not walk in darkness, but will have the light of life.

John 8:12

38   You will know the truth, and the truth will make you free.

John 8:32

39   I am the door; if any one enters by me, he will be saved.

John 10:9

40   I came that they may have life, and have it abundantly.

John 10:10

41   I am the good shepherd; I know my own and my own know me; and I have other sheep that are not of this fold; I must bring them also, and they will heed my voice. So there shall be one flock, one shepherd.

John 10:14, 16

42 A new commandment I give to you, that you love one another; even as I have loved you, that you also love one another. By this all men will know that you are my disciples, if you have love for one another.

John 13:34–35

43. Let not your hearts be troubled; believe in God, believe also in me.

John 14:1

44 In my Father's house are many rooms; if it were not so, would I have told you that I go to prepare a place for you? And when I go and prepare a place for you, I will come again and will take you to myself that where I am you may be also.

John 14:2–3

45 I am the way, and the truth, and the life; no one comes to the Father, but by me.

John 14:6

46 Truly, truly, I say to you, he who believes in me will also do the works that I do; and greater works than these will he do, because I go to the Father.

John 14:12

47 If you love me, you will keep my commandments.

John 14:15

48 I will pray the Father, and he will give you another Counselor, to be with you for ever.

John 14:16

49 He who has my commandments and keeps them, he it is who loves me; and he who loves me will be loved by my Father, and I will love him and manifest myself to him.

John 14:21

50 I am the vine, you are the branches. He who abides in me, and I in him, he it is that bears fruit, for apart from me you can do nothing.

John 15:5

51 If you abide in me, and my words abide in you, ask whatever you will, and it shall be done for you.

John 15:7

52   As the Father has loved me, so have I loved you; abide in my love.

John 15:9

53   This is my commandment, that you love one another as I have loved you.

John 15:12

54   Greater love has no man than this, that a man lay down his life for his friends.

John 15:13

55   You are my friends if you do what I command you.

John 15:14

56   No longer do I call you servants, for the servant does not know what his master is doing; but I have called you friends, for all that I have heard from my Father I have made known to you.

John 15:15

57   You did not choose me, but I chose you and appointed you that you should go and bear fruit and that your fruit should abide; so that whatever you ask the Father in my name, he may give it to you.

John 15:16

58   I have yet many things to say to you, but you cannot bear them now.

John 16:12

59   I have said this to you, that in me you may have peace. In the world you have tribulation; but be of good cheer, I have overcome the world.

John 16:33

60   This is eternal life, that they know thee the only true God, and Jesus Christ whom thou hast sent.

John 17:3

61   God shows his love for us in that while we were yet sinners Christ died for us.

Romans 5:8

62   For all who are led by the Spirit of God are sons of God. For you did not receive the spirit of slavery to fall back into fear, but you have received the spirit of sonship. When we cry, "Abba! Father!" it is the Spirit himself bearing witness with our spirit that we are children of God.

Romans 8:14–16

63   Who shall separate us from the love of Christ? Shall tribulation, or distress, or persecution, or famine, or nakedness, or peril, or sword? No, in all these things we are more than conquerors through him who loved us. For I am sure that neither death, nor life, nor angels, nor principalities, nor things present, nor things to come, nor powers, nor height, nor depth, nor anything else in all creation, will be able to separate us from the love of God in Christ Jesus our Lord.

Romans 8:35, 37–39

64   I appeal to you therefore, brethren, by the mercies of God, to present your bodies as a living sacrifice, holy and acceptable to God, which is your spiritual worship.

Romans 12:1

65   If we have sown spiritual good among you, is it too much if we reap your material benefits?

I Corinthians 9:11

66   In the same way, the Lord commanded that those who proclaim the gospel should get their living by the gospel.

I Corinthians 9:14

67   He who sows sparingly will also reap sparingly, and he who sows bountifully will also reap bountifully. Each one must do as he has made up his mind, not reluctantly or under compulsion, for God loves a cheerful giver.

II Corinthians 9:6–7

68   So then, as we have opportunity, let us do good to all men, and especially to those who are of the household of faith.

Galatians 6:10

69   For this reason I bow my knees before the Father, from whom every family in heaven and on earth is named, that according to the riches of his glory he may grant you to be strengthened with might through his Spirit in the inner man, and that Christ may dwell in your hearts through faith; that you, being rooted and grounded in love, may have power to comprehend with all the saints what is the breadth and length and height and depth, and to know the love of Christ which surpasses knowledge, that you may be filled with all the fulness of God.

Ephesians 4:14–19

70   The saying is sure and worthy of full acceptance, that Christ Jesus came into the world to save sinners.

I Timothy 1:15

71   For we brought nothing into the world, and we cannot take anything out of the world.

I Timothy 6:7

72   Do your best to present yourself to God as one approved, a workman who has no need to be ashamed, rightly handling the word of truth.

II Timothy 2:15

73   For God is not so unjust as to overlook your work and the love which you showed for his sake in serving the saints, as you still do.

Hebrews 6:10

74   If we walk in the light, as he is in the light, we have fellowship with one another, and the blood of Jesus his Son cleanses us from all sin.

I John 1:7

75   If we confess our sins, he is faithful and just, and will forgive our sins and cleanse us from all unrighteousness.

I John 1:9

76   My little children, I am writing this to you so that you may not sin; but if any one does sin, we have an advocate with the Father, Jesus Christ the righteous; and he is the expiation for our sins, and not for ours only but also for the

sins of the whole world. And by this we may be sure that we know him, if we keep his commandments.

I John 2:1–3

77   See what love the Father has given us, that we should be called children of God; and so we are. The reason why the world does not know us is that it did not know him. Beloved, we are God's children now; it does not yet appear what we shall be, but we know that when he appears we shall be like him, for we shall see him as he is. And every one who thus hopes in him purifies himself as he is pure.

I John 3:1–3

78   Beloved, let us love one another; for love is of God, and he who loves is born of God and knows God. He who does not love does not know God; for God is love.

I John 4:7–8

79   There is no fear in love, but perfect love casts out fear. For fear has to do with punishment, and he who fears is not perfected in love. We love, because he first loved us.

I John 4:18–19

80   Behold, I stand at the door and knock; if any one hears my voice and opens the door, I will come in to him and eat with him, and he with me.

Revelation 3:20

XIV

Invitations
to
Communion

1   Ye who do truly and earnestly repent you of your sins, and are in love and charity with your neighbors, and intend to lead a new life, following the commandments of God, and walking from henceforth in his holy ways; Draw near with faith, and take this holy Sacrament to your comfort; and make your humble confession to Almighty God.

The Book of Common Prayer

2   Come to this sacred Table, not because you must, but because you may: come to testify, not that you are righteous, but that you sincerely love our Lord Jesus Christ, and desire to be His true disciples: come, not because you are strong, but because you are weak; not because you have any claim on Heaven's high rewards, but because in your frailty and sin you stand in constant need of Heaven's mercy and help; come, not to express an opinion, but to seek a Presence and pray for a Spirit.

Devotional Services

3   The Table of the Lord is spread.
Come, for all things are now ready.
Dearly beloved: this Table of the Lord is open to all our fellow-Christians; and, although none should draw near to this sacrament impenitent or wilfully unbelieving, in the name of our Lord Jesus Christ, we affectionately invite all who are sincerely seeking him, and all who are wearied of their sin and doubt, to come to the Lord's Table, in the assurance which he himself has given us:
Him that cometh unto me, I will in no wise cast out.

Divine Service, (adapted)

4   Dearly beloved, as we draw near to the Lord's Table to celebrate the Holy Communion of the Body and Blood of Christ, we are gratefully to remember that this sacrament was instituted as a memorial of his undying love for us, as a seal of our bond of union with him and with each other as members of his mystical Body, and as a pledge of his faithfulness unto them that are called to the marriage-supper of the Lamb.

Book of Common Order, Canada

5   And now that the Supper of the Lord is spread before you, lift up your minds and hearts above all selfish fears and cares; let this bread and wine be to you the witnesses and signs of the grace of our Lord Jesus Christ, the love of God, and the communion of the Holy Spirit. Before the Throne of the heavenly Father and the Cross of the Redeemer make your humble confession of sin, consecrate your lives to the Christian obedience and service, and pray for strength to do and to bear the holy and blessed will of God.

Devotional Services

6   Dearly beloved: it is right that we who would come to the Communion of the Lord's Supper should take to heart the mystery of the Lord's Table.

The mystery is this: in obedience to the Father's will and in infinite love for us, the Good Shepherd has laid down his life for the sheep; he who was without sin has died for sinners; the High Priest has offered himself as the perfect sacrifice. Thus, by his death, he has done away with all that stood in the way of our fellowship with God the Father, that we may assuredly be his children, upheld by his love, guided by him all the days of our life, and rejoicing in the hope of glory.

"The Lord's Supper," Church of South India

7   We are taught in the Holy Scriptures not to forsake the assembling of ourselves together, to meet with God and learn from him.

Wherefore I say to each one of you: Thy Lord is here to meet thee. Remove now earthly thoughts from thy mind, for the place whereon thou standest is holy ground.

Let thy praise be from thy heart, and do not in thy praying mock the Lord with idle thoughts or empty speech. Read reverently his holy Word, and do thy part to understand the message he may send.

And to this end, I pray you every one to ask his grace and help—first, for yourselves, that you may fix your minds on him and then for us all, that, thus praying for one another, we may be greatly blest.

A Book of Services and Prayers

8   Dearly beloved, we are come together in obedience to our Lord's command for this sacred memorial of the Lord's Supper. We invite to its blessing and fellowship all disciples of the Lord Jesus who have confessed him before men and desire to serve him with sincere hearts. This is not our Table but the Table of our Lord.

The Book of Common Worship

9   Dearly beloved, in the holy quiet of this hour let us draw nigh to him who heareth prayer; let us remember he listeneth more to our hearts than to our words, and that we are the children of his love. As we bow before him may we be delivered from blindness and prejudice and from fear. May the God of all grace so cleanse our hearts and so order our minds that they shall be open to the kindling touch of the mysterious Spirit of him before we wait.

The Pilgrim Hymnal

10   Dearly Beloved, as we draw near to the Lord's Table, let us gratefully remember that our Lord instituted this sacrament for the perpetual memory of his dying for our sakes and the pledge of his undying love; as a bond for our union with him and with each other as members of his mystical Body; as a seal of his promises to us and a renewal of our obedience to him; and for the blessed assurance of his presence with us who are gathered here in his name.

The Book of Common Worship

11   Although you may feel that you have not perfect faith, and do not serve God as you ought; yet if, by God's grace, you are heartily sorry for your sins and infirmities, and earnestly desire to withstand all unbelief, and to keep all His commandments, be assured that your remaining imperfections do not prevent you from being received of God in mercy, and so made worthy partakers of his heavenly food.

Book of Common Order, 1896

12   Dearly beloved, we have come apart into this house of praise and prayer to renew our souls at the fountains of life. We are all children of the household of God, fellow-travellers toward his promised rest. With humble hearts and with hope-

ful spirits let us offer up our prayers to him who, though he dwelleth on high, is yet very present, and never faileth to listen to all who call upon him out of their need and hope and love.

The Pilgrim Hymnal

13 We come not to this supper as righteous in ourselves, but we come to seek our life in Christ, acknowledging that we lie in the midst of death. Let us, then, look upon this sacrament as a remedy for those who are sick, and consider that the worthiness our Lord requireth of us is that we be truly sorry for our sins, and find our joy and salvation in Him. United in Him who is holy, even our Lord Jesus Christ, we are accepted of the Father, and invited to partake of these holy things which are for holy persons.

Book of Common Order, 1896

14 Dearly beloved, as we are met to celebrate the Supper of our Lord, let us earnestly consider our great need of having our comfort and strength renewed in this our earthly pilgrimage and warfare; and especially how necessary it is that we come to the Lord's Table with knowledge, faith, repentance and love; with hearts hungering and thirsting after him. Therefore, in the holy quiet of this hour, let us draw nigh to him who heareth prayer, remembering that he listeneth more to our hearts than to our words. As we thus come with an offering of penitence, of love, and of teachableness, may we find grace to help in time of need, and rest and refreshment unto our souls.

The Pilgrim Hymnal

15 Let us with humility and thanksgiving come to this Communion. Our Lord Jesus Christ has set the table. He who loved us and gave himself up for us invites us to partake, hence the Lord's Supper cannot be the special possession of any person or group. If with all our heart we love the Lord and desire to do this, as he said, "In remembrance of me," then it is our gracious privilege to share in this Communion with him. Let us examine our hearts and prepare our minds that we may truly feed on living bread.

Christian Worship: A Service Book

16   Dearly beloved, as we are now about to celebrate the Holy Communion of the body and blood of Christ, let us consider how St. Paul exhorteth all persons to examine themselves before they eat of that bread, and drink of that cup. For as the benefit is great, if with a truly penitent heart and lively faith we receive that holy sacrament (for then we spiritually eat the flesh of Christ, and drink His blood; then we dwell in Christ and Christ in us; we are one with Christ and Christ with us), so is the danger great if we receive the same unworthily. For he that eateth and drinketh unworthily, eateth and drinketh judgment to himself, not discerning the Lord's body.

Book of Common Order, 1896

17   Remember, the worthiness which our Lord requires from us is that we should be truly sorry for our sins, and find our joy and salvation in him. For we come to this Supper, not as righteous in ourselves, but trusting in the righteousness of Christ our Savior. Acknowledging that, even in the midst of this sinful life, we are united with him who is holy, even our Lord Jesus Christ, we are accepted by the Father, and invited to partake of this holy sacrament.

"The Lord's Supper," Church of South India

18   How through this Sacrament of simple things
The great God burns His way,
I know not—He is there.
The silent air
Is pulsing with the presence of His grace,
Almost I feel a face
Bend o'er me as I kneel.

G. A. Studdert-Kennedy

19   I warn all who are not of the number of the faithful, all who live in any sin against their knowledge or their conscience, charging them that they profane not this holy table.
And yet this is not pronounced to exclude any penitent person, how grievous soever his sins have been, but only such as continue in sin without repentance.

Examine your own consciences, therefore, to know whether you truly repent of your sins, and whether, trusting in God's mercy, and seeking your whole salvation in Jesus Christ, you are resolved to follow in holiness, and to live in peace and charity with all men.

If you have this testimony in your hearts before God, be assured that your sins are forgiven through the perfect merit of Jesus Christ our Lord; and I bid you, in His name, to His holy table.

Book of Common Order, 1896

20   We have come together to worship God:
            to thank him for his goodness, and to praise him for
                his glory
            to confess our sins, and to hear his Word;
            to ask his blessing, for ourselves and others.
        We come to meditate on things unseen, and to draw
                strength from things eternal:
            to seek courage for our duty, and guidance for our
                way;
            to remember that God made us, and that we find
                our life in him.
        We come in the name of the Lord Jesus:
            who went, as his custom was, into the synagogue
                on the sabbath day;
            who taught us to pray;
            who promised his presence to the two or three;
            his rest to the heavy-laden; and his peace to all who
                love and trust him.
        Let us, therefore, turn to him in prayer, who is not
            far from any one of us.

A Book of Services and Prayers

21   This is the day which the Lord hath made;
            we will rejoice and be glad in it.
        This is the feast which the Lord hath spread;
            we will draw near and partake of it.
        This is the Body and Blood of Christ;
            let us go forth in his name.

Francis C. Lightbourne

22   We come, not because we are worthy; not for any righteousness of ours; for we have grievously sinned and fallen short of what, but for God's help, we might have been.

We come, not because there is any magic in partaking of the symbols of Christ's body and blood.

We come, not from a sense of duty that is unacquainted with deep appreciation for this blessed means of grace—the highest privilege of Christian worship.

We come, because Christ bids us come. It is His table, and He extends the invitation.

We come because it is a memorial to Him, as often as it is done in remembrance of Him. Here is a vivid portrayal of the redeeming sacrifice of the Christ of Calvary. His matchless life, His victorious sufferings, and His faithfulness even unto death, are brought to mind, and we bow humbly before Him and worship.

We come because in contemplation of the Father and His Son our Saviour, we are moved to thanksgiving for so great a salvation.

We come because in this encounter with the Saviour we are made to feel the wrongness of our sins, base desires, unchristian motives, hurtful attitudes, vain ambitions, and the things we have done which we ought not to have done and the things we have failed to do which God expected us to do. We acknowledge our utter unworthiness and walk again the painful, but necessary, path of repentance.

We come because forgiveness comes with true repentance. We arise with the assurance of pardon, rejoicing in the opportunity of a new beginning.

We come because we want to experience high communion with God the Father, revealed in Jesus Christ, and ever present in the Person of the Holy Spirit. And, having fellowship with Him, we are drawn closer to all who kneel with us at the altar and, indeed, we became conscious of our kinship with all men everywhere who claim our Christ as Saviour, the Holy universal fellowship of believers.

We come because we arise from the Lord's table with new strength, courage, poise, and power to live for Him who died for us.

Author Unknown

23   At Holy Communion we are invited to the Lord's Table with the condition that we repent of our sins; that we are in love and charity with our neighbors, and intend to live a new life. Then we are bidden to draw near in faith that God will see us when we are a long way off, in faith that with him we shall eat and drink and be merry, knowing that we have been lost but are found.   George W. Barrett

24   Dearly beloved, we are assembled and met together to render thanks to Almighty God, our heavenly Father, for the great benefits that we have received at his hands;
to set forth his most worthy praise;
to acknowledge and confess our sins;
to hear his most holy Word;
and to ask those things which are requisite and necessary, as well for the body as the soul.
Let us, therefore, draw near to God with a humble, lowly, penitent, and obedient heart; to the end that we may obtain forgiveness and grace, and adore him for this infinite goodness and mercy.
A Book of Services and Prayers

25   He was the Word, that spake it:
He took the bread and break it;
And what that Word did make it,
I do believe and take it.

26   Brethren, we have come to hear God's most holy Word, and to receive the body and blood of the Lord. Let us therefore kneel and examine ourselves in silence, seeking God's grace that we may draw near to him with repentance and faith.   Order of Service, South India

27   As our Lord offers to us these blessings of our redemption, so he seeks to change us that we may become like him. He pours his love into our hearts that we may learn to love him, to love one another, and also to love our enemies. In the power of his resurrection he wants us to crucify the old man with its lusts, and to walk in newness of life. In the fellowship of his sufferings, he wants us to bear trials and tribulations patiently, to the glory of his name.
"The Lord's Supper," Church of South India

XV

Benedictions
and
Prayers at Close
of Worship

This section contains *Closing Sentences, Scriptural and General Ascriptions of Praise,* and *Benedictions.* In most instances the distinctions are so finely drawn that it is difficult to distinguish one from the other, and they are often used interchangeably at the close of worship. *Closing Sentences* are commonly scriptural verses, or prayers, relating to the general theme or sermon of the day. For instance, if the subject relates to brotherhood, the Closing Sentence might read: "May the Lord who made of one blood all men to dwell on the face of the earth enable you to dwell together in unity." Closing Sentences may be followed by an appropriate Ascription of Praise to God. The *Benediction* is not a general prayer, but should always be either a Scriptural Ascription of Praise to the deity, or a blessing pronounced upon the people.

A. FROM THE OLD TESTAMENT

1   The Lord watch between you and me, when we are absent one from the other.

Genesis 31:49

2   The Lord bless you and keep you:
The Lord make his face to shine upon you, and be gracious to you:
The Lord lift up his countenance upon you, and give you peace.

Numbers 6:24–26

3   The Lord our God be with us, as he was with our fathers; may he not leave us or forsake us; that he may incline our hearts to him, to walk in all his ways, and to keep his commandments, his statutes, and his ordinances, which he commanded our fathers.

I Kings 8:57–58

4   Let your heart therefore be wholly true to the Lord our God, walking in his statutes and keeping his commandments, as at this day.

I Kings 8:61

5   Blessed art thou, O Lord, the God of Israel our father, for ever and ever. Thine, O Lord, is the greatness, and the power, and the glory, and the victory, and the majesty for all that is in the heavens and in the earth is thine; thine is the kingdom, O Lord, and thou art exalted as head above all.

I Chronicles 29:10–11

6   O Lord, the God of Abraham, Isaac, and Israel, our fathers, keep for ever such purposes and thoughts in the hearts of thy people, and direct their hearts toward thee.

I Chronicles 29:18

7   Let the words of my mouth and the meditation of my heart be acceptable in thy sight,
O Lord, my rock and my redeemer.

Psalms 19:14

8   O save thy people, and bless thy heritage;
    be thou their shepherd, and carry them for ever.

Psalms 28:9

9   May God be gracious to us and bless us
    and make his face to shine upon us,
    that thy way be known upon earth,
        thy saving power among all nations.
    Let the peoples praise thee, O God;
        let all the peoples praise thee!

Psalms 67:1–3

10   Let thy work be manifest to thy servants,
    and thy glorious power to their children.
    Let the favor of the Lord our God be upon us,
        and establish thou the work of our hands upon us,
        yea, the work of our hands establish thou it.

Psalms 90:16–17

11   The Lord is your keeper;
    the Lord is your shade
    on your right hand.
    The Lord will keep you from all evil;
    he will keep your life.
    The Lord will keep
        your going out and your coming in
        from this time forth and for evermore.

Psalms 121:5, 7–8

B. FROM THE NEW TESTAMENT

12   Lord, now lettest thou thy servant depart in peace,
    according to thy word;
    for mine eyes have seen thy salvation
    which thou hast prepared in the presence of all
    peoples, a light for revelation to the Gentiles,
        and for glory to thy people Israel.

Luke 2:29–32

13   And now I commend you to God and to the word of
his grace, which is able to build you up and to give you the
inheritance among all those who are sanctified.

Acts 20:32

14   Grace to you and peace from God our Father and the Lord Jesus Christ.

Romans 1:7

15   May the God of steadfastness and encouragement grant you to live in such harmony with one another, in accord with Christ Jesus, that together you may with one voice glorify the God and Father of our Lord Jesus Christ.

Romans 15:5–6

16   May the God of hope fill you with all joy and peace in believing, so that by the power of the Holy Spirit you may abound in hope.

Romans 15:13

17   The God of peace be with you all. Amen.

Romans 15:33

18   Now to him who is able to strengthen you according to my gospel and the preaching of Jesus Christ, according to the revelation of the mystery which was kept secret for long ages but is now disclosed and through the prophetic writings is made known to all nations, according to the command of the eternal God, to bring about obedience to the faith—to the only wise God be glory for evermore through Jesus Christ! Amen.

Romans 16:25–27

19   The grace of the Lord Jesus be with you.

I Corinthians 16:23

20   Blessed be the God and Father of our Lord Jesus Christ, the Father of mercies and God of all comfort, who comforts us in all our affliction, so that we may be able to comfort those who are in any affliction, with the comfort with which we ourselves are comforted by God.

II Corinthians 1:3–4

21   God is able to provide you with every blessing in abundance, so that you may always have enough of everything and may provide in abundance for every good work.

II Corinthians 9:8

22   Finally, brethren, farewell. Mend your ways, heed my appeal, agree with one another, live in peace, and the God of love and peace will be with you.

II Corinthians 13:11

23   The grace of the Lord Jesus Christ and the love of God and the fellowship of the Holy Spirit be with you all.

II Corinthians 13:14

24   Grace to you and peace from God the Father and our Lord Jesus Christ, who gave himself for our sins to deliver us from the present evil age, according to the will of our God and Father; to whom be the glory for ever and ever. Amen.

Galatians 1:3–5

25   The grace of our Lord Jesus Christ be with your spirit, brethren. Amen.

Galatians 6:18

26   Blessed be the God and Father of our Lord Jesus Christ, who has blessed us in Christ with every spiritual blessing in the heavenly places, even as he chose us in him before the foundation of the world, that we should be holy and blameless before him.

Ephesians 1:3–4

27   According to the riches of his glory he may grant you to be strengthened with might through his Spirit in the inner man, and that Christ may dwell in your hearts through faith; that you, being rooted and grounded in love, may have power to comprehend with all the saints what is the breadth and length and height and depth, and to know the love of Christ which surpasses knowledge, that you may be filled with all the fulness of God.

Ephesians 3:16–19

28   Now to him who by the power at work within us is able to do far more abundantly than all that we ask or think, and to him be glory in the church and in Christ Jesus to all generations, for ever and ever. Amen.

Ephesians 3:20–21

29   Peace . . . and love with faith, from God the Father and the Lord Jesus Christ. Grace be with all who love our Lord Jesus Christ with love undying.

Ephesians 6:23–24

30   And the peace of God, which passes all understanding, will keep your hearts and your minds in Christ Jesus.

Philippians 4:7

31   Finally, brethren, whatever is true, whatever is honorable, whatever is just, whatever is pure, whatever is lovely, whatever is gracious, if there is any excellence, if there is anything worthy of praise, think about these things.

Philippians 4:8

32   May you be filled with the knowledge of his will in all spiritual wisdom and understanding, to lead a life worthy of the Lord, fully pleasing to him, bearing fruit in every good work and increasing in the knowledge of God.

Colossians 1:9–10

33   May you be strengthened with all power, according to his glorious might, for all endurance and patience with joy, giving thanks to the Father, who has qualified us to share in the inheritance of the saints in light.

Colossians 1:11–12

34   Put on then, as God's chosen ones, holy and beloved, compassion, kindness, lowliness, meekness, and patience, forbearing one another and, if one has a complaint against another, forgiving each other; as the Lord has forgiven you, so you also must forgive. And above all these put on love, which binds everything together in perfect harmony.

Colossians 3:12–14

35   And let the peace of Christ rule in your hearts, to which indeed you were called in the one body. And be thankful.

Colossians 3:15

36   Let the word of Christ dwell in you richly, as you teach and admonish one another in all wisdom, and as you

sing psalms and hymns and spiritual songs with thankfulness in your hearts of God.

Colossians 3:16

37   And whatever you do, in word or deed, do everything in the name of the Lord Jesus giving thanks to God the Father through him.

Colossians 3:17

38   May the Lord make you increase and abound in love to one another and to all men, as we do to you, so that he may establish your hearts unblamable in holiness before our God and Father.

I Thessalonians 3:12–13

39   May the God of peace himself sanctify you wholly; and may your spirit and soul and body be kept sound and blameless at the coming of our Lord Jesus Christ.

I Thessalonians 5:23

40   Grace to you and peace from God the Father and the Lord Jesus Christ.

II Thessalonians 1:2

41   We always pray for you, that our God may make you worthy of his call, and may fulfil every good resolve and work of faith by his power, so that the name of our Lord Jesus may be glorified in you, and you in him, according to the grace of our God and the Lord Jesus Christ.

II Thessalonians 1:11–12

42   Now may our Lord Jesus Christ himself, and God our Father, who loved us and gave us eternal comfort and good hope through grace, comfort your hearts and establish them in every good work and word.

II Thessalonians 2:16–17

43   Now may the Lord of peace himself give you peace at all times in all ways. The Lord be with you all.

II Thessalonians 3:16

44   To the King of ages, immortal, invisible, the only God, be honor and glory for ever and ever. Amen.

I Timothy 1:17

45   Aim at righteousness, godliness, faith, love, stead-fastness, gentleness. Fight the good fight of the faith; take hold of the eternal life to which you were called when you made the good confession in the presence of many witnesses.

I Timothy 6:11–12

46   Grace, mercy, and peace from God the Father and Christ Jesus our Lord.

II Timothy 1:2

47   Do your best to present yourself to God as one approved, a workman who has no need to be ashamed, rightly handling the word of truth.

II Timothy 2:15

48   Now may the God of peace who brought again from the dead our Lord Jesus, the great shepherd of the sheep, by the blood of the eternal covenant, equip you with everything good that you may do his will, working in you that which is pleasing in his sight, through Jesus Christ; to whom be glory for ever and ever. Amen.

Hebrews 13:20-21

49   Blessed be the God and Father of our Lord Jesus Christ! . . . without having seen him you love him; though you do not now see him you believe in him and rejoice with unutterable and exalted joy.

I Peter 1:1, 8

50   Having purified your souls by your obedience to the truth for a sincere love of the brethren, love one another earnestly from the heart.

I Peter 1:22

51   As each has received a gift, employ it for one another, as good stewards of God's varied grace: whoever renders service, as one who renders it by the strength which God supplies; in order that in everything God may be glorified through Jesus Christ. To him belong glory and dominion for ever and ever. Amen.

I Peter 4:10–11

52   The God of all grace, who has called you to his eternal glory in Christ, will himself restore, establish, and strengthen you. To him be the dominion for ever and ever. Amen.

I Peter 5:10–11

53   May grace and peace be multiplied to you in the knowledge of God and of Jesus our Lord.

II Peter 1:2

54   Grow in the grace and knowledge of our Lord and Savior Jesus Christ. To him be the glory both now and to the day of eternity. Amen.

II Peter 3:18

55   Grace, mercy, and peace will be with us, from God the Father and from Jesus Christ the Father's Son, in truth and love.

II John 1:3

56   Beloved, I pray that all may go well with you and that you may be in health; I know that it is well with your soul.

III John 1:2

57   To those who are called, beloved in God the Father and kept for Jesus Christ: May mercy, peace, and love be multiplied to you.

Jude 1:1–2

58   But you beloved, build yourselves up on your most holy faith; pray in the Holy Spirit; keep yourselves in the love of God; wait for the mercy of our Lord Jesus Christ unto eternal life.

Jude 1:20–21

59   Now to him who is able to keep you from falling and to present you without blemish before the presence of his glory with rejoicing, to the only God, our Saviour through Jesus Christ our Lord be glory, majesty, dominion, and authority, before all time and now and for ever. Amen.

Jude 1:24–25

60   Grace to you and peace from him who is and who was and who is to come, and from the seven spirits who are before his throne, and from Jesus Christ the faithful witness, the firstborn of the dead, and the ruler of kings on earth. To him who loves us and has freed us from our sins by his blood and made us a kingdom, priests to his God and Father, to him be glory and dominion for ever and ever. Amen.

Revelation 1:4–6

61   "Amen! Blessing and glory and wisdom and thanksgiving and honor and power and might be to our God for ever and ever! Amen.

Revelation 7:12

62   The grace of our Lord Jesus Christ be with you all.

Revelation 22:21, KJV

C. FROM OTHER SOURCES

63   God be gracious unto you . . . and give you all an heart to serve him, and to do his will, with a good courage and a willing mind; and open your heart in his law and commandments, and send you peace, and hear your prayers, and be at one with you.

II Macabees 1:2–5

64   May He, whose love and understanding are around you, bless you and fill your hearts with peace.

65   Now may the peace of God
Be above you and around you;
Beneath you and within you;
May it shine through you
Until there is the peace of God on earth.

66   And now may the courage of the early morning's dawning, and the strength of the eternal hills, and the peace of the evening's ending, and the love of God, be in your hearts now and forevermore.

67   Grant, O Lord, that our eyes which have looked upon Thy cross may ever look to Thee for light and guidance; that

our tongues which have sung Thy praise may ever speak the truth in love; that our ears which have heard Thy voice may be closed to all unworthy voices; that our feet which have walked in this Thy church may ever walk in the paths that lead to righteousness and peace; and grant that our hearts which have here waited before Thee may be ever open to Thy coming; through Jesus Christ our Lord.

The Liturgy of Malabar

68   Now the God of patience and consolation grant you to be likeminded one toward another according to Christ Jesus; that ye may with one mind and one mouth glorify God our Father and the Lord Jesus Christ.

69   Father, give thy benediction,
      Give thy peace before we part;
      Still our minds with truth's conviction
      Calm with trust each anxious heart.

Samuel Longfellow, 1819–1892

70   Grace and peace be multiplied unto you through the knowledge of God, and of Jesus our Lord; according as his divine power has given us all things that pertain unto life and godliness, through the knowledge of him that hath both called us to glory and virtue.

71   Be Lord:
      within me to strengthen me,
      without me to guard me,
      over me to shelter me,
      beneath me to stablish me,
      before me to guide me,
      after me to forward me,
      round about me to secure me.

Lancelot Andrewes, 1555–1626

72   Now may the spirit which was in Jesus be in you also, enabling you to know the truth and to do the will of God, and to abide in His peace.

73   The Almighty God, Father of our Lord and Saviour, Jesus Christ, mercifully protect you, strengthen you and guide you.

Melanchthon, 1497–1560

74   May God's spirit guide us as we seek to learn and do His will; may His peace possess our souls; and His kingdom come on earth.

75   May he (God) bless you with all good and keep you from all evil; may he give light to your heart with loving wisdom and be gracious to you with eternal knowledge; may he lift up his loving countenance to you for eternal peace.

Dead Sea Scrolls

76   May the Love which is greater than ourselves, which is above ourselves, and to which we give ourselves, be with us now and forever.

77   Lord, make me an instrument of Thy peace; where there is hatred, let me sow love; where there is injury, pardon; where there is doubt, faith; where there is despair, hope; where there is darkness, light; and where there is sadness, hope.

O Divine Master, grant that I may not so much seek to be consoled as to console; to be understood, as to understand; to be loved, as to love; for it is in giving that we receive, it is in pardoning that we are pardoned, and it is in dying that we are born to eternal life.

St. Francis of Assisi, 1182–1226

78   And now to the Father, Son, and Holy Ghost, three Persons and one God, be ascribed by us and by the whole church, as is most due, the kingdom, the power, and the glory, for ever and ever.

79   Commending you to Him who can go with me and stay with you and be everywhere for good, I bid you an affectionate farewell.

Abraham Lincoln, 1809–1865

80   May Christ's wonderful, never-failing kindness, God's saving and sustaining love, and the Holy Spirit's gift of fellowship with God and the church give you every blessing and aid.

81   Extolled and hallowed be the Name of God throughout the world; and may he speedily establish his kingdom of righteousness on earth.

Union Prayer Book

82　Blessed be the Name of the Lord for ever. Peace be with you all. In the peace of Christ let us depart. Lord, bless us.

Liturgy of St. James, 1st Century

83　Depart in peace in the Name of the Lord. The love of God and the Father, the grace of the Son of our Lord Jesus Christ, the communion and gift of the Holy Ghost, be with us all, now and ever, and to ages of ages. Blessed be the name of the Lord.

Liturgy of St. Mark, 1st Century

84　Be blessed by the grace of the Holy Spirit. Go in peace, and may the Lord be with you all.

Liturgy of the Armenians

85　May our Lord Jesus Christ be near you to defend you, within you to refresh you, around you to preserve you, before you to guide you, behind you to justify you, above you to bless you: Who liveth and reigneth with the Father and the Holy Ghost, God for evermore.

Latin Prayer, 10th Century

86　Let the earth bless the Lord: yea, let it praise him, and magnify him for ever. Let us bless the Father, and the Son, and the Holy Ghost: praise him, and magnify him for ever.

Benedicite

87　Eternal God, thou hast shown us what is good and what thou dost require of us: to do justly, to love mercy, and to walk humbly with thee. Great peace have they who love thy Law, and nothing can offend them; Lord, give strength unto thy people; O God, bless thy people with peace.

Union Prayer Book

88　The Lord go forth with you, from this his holy house; and send down upon you his love and light and calm, wherein ye may continually dwell and worship with him forevermore.

William E. Gladstone, 1809–1898

89   God the Father, God the Son, God the Holy Ghost, bless, preserve, and keep you. The Lord mercifully with his favour look upon you and fill you with all spiritual benediction and grace; that ye may so live together in this life, that in the world to come you may have life everlasting.

The Book of Common Prayer

90   Bless all who worship Thee, from the rising of the sun unto the going down of the same. Of thy goodness give us, with Thy love inspire us, by Thy Spirit guide us, by Thy power protect us, in Thy mercy receive us, now and always.

Ancient Collects

91   Lord, dismiss us with Thy blessing:
Fill our hearts with joy and peace:
Let us each, Thy love possessing,
Triumph in redeeming grace;
O refresh us, O refresh us,
Trav'ling through this wilderness.

John Fawcett, 1739–1817

92   Saviour, again to Thy dear name we raise
With one accord our parting hymn of praise;
We stand to bless Thee ere our worship cease;
Then, lowly kneeling, wait Thy word of peace.

John Ellerton, 1826–1893

93   O Thou who hast gathered us out of many places and by the grace of Thy spirit bound us together into the fellowship of the Christian church, bless us as we go forth. Prepare us for the coming of Thy Holy Spirit into our lives and fill our hearts with Thy Goodness.

94   Sweet Saviour, bless us ere we go,
Thy word into our minds instil,
And make our lukewarm hearts to glow
With lowly love and fervent will.
Through life's long day and death's dark night,
O gentle Jesus, be our light.

Frederick W. Faber, 1814–1863

95   May the souls of the faithful, through the mercy of God, rest in peace; and may light perpetual shine upon them; and may the grace of our Lord Jesus Christ, and the love of God, and the fellowship of the Holy Ghost, be with us all evermore.

96   O God, bless our homes, our families, friends, and neighbors, and give us thankful hearts for all thy mercies.

97   The peace of God which passeth all understanding keep your hearts and minds in the knowledge and love of God, and of His Son Jesus Christ our Lord, and the blessing of God Almighty, the Father, the Son, and the Holy Ghost, be amongst you and remain with you always.

Book of Common Prayer

98   Unto God's gracious mercy and protection we commit you. The Lord bless you and keep you. The Lord make his face to shine upon you, and be gracious unto you. The Lord lift up his countenance upon you, and give you peace in your going out and your coming in, in your lying down and your rising up, in your labor and your leisure, in your laughter and your tears, until you come to stand before Him in that day to which there is no sunset and no dawn.

G. A. Studdert-Kennedy, 1883–1929

99   Lighten our darkness, we beseech Thee, O Lord, and by Thy great mercy defend us from all perils of this night; for the love of Thine only Son, our Saviour, Jesus Christ.

Book of Common Prayer

100   May the blessing of God Almighty, the Father, the Son, and the Holy Ghost, rest upon us and upon all our work and worship done in His Name. May He give us light to guide us, courage to support us, and love to unite us, now and forevermore.

101   O Thou who art the Creator of all life and the Ruler of the sea, give peace and charm unto our hearts, even in the midst of storm and tempest, for our trust is in Thee. Bring us in good time unto the desired haven.

Book of Common Worship

102   God Almighty, bless us with His Holy Spirit; guard us in our going out and our coming in; keep us ever steadfast in His faith; free from sin and safe from danger; through Jesus Christ our Lord.

A Chain of Prayer Across the Ages

103   Unto God the Father, the Son and the Holy Ghost be ascribed in the church all honor and glory, might, majesty, dominion, and blessing, now, henceforth, and forever.

Book of Common Worship

104   To God the Father, who loved us, and made us accepted in the Beloved:
To God the Son, who loved us, and loosed us from sin by his blood:
To God the Holy Spirit, who sheddeth the love of God abroad in our hearts:
To the one true God be all love and all glory for time and eternity.

A Book of Services and Prayers

105   Now unto the God of all grace, who hath called us unto his eternal glory by Christ Jesus, be all power and dominion for ever and ever.

Book of Common Worship

106   Go forth into the world and peace: be of good courage; hold fast to that which is good: render to no man evil for evil; strengthen the fainthearted; support the weak; help the afflicted; honour all men; love and serve the Lord, rejoicing in the power of the Holy Spirit.
And the blessing of God Almighty, the Father, the Son, and the Holy Spirit, be upon you and remain with you for ever.

The Book of Common Prayer

107   Unto him who loved us, and washed us from our sins in his own blood, and hath made us kings and priests unto God, his Father, to him be glory and dominion for ever and ever.

Book of Common Worship

108   May the strength of God pilot us. May the power of God preserve us. May the wisdom of God instruct us. May the hand of God protect us. May the way of God direct us. May the shield of God defend us now and forever.

St. Patrick, 389–461

109   And now may the blessing of the Lord rest and remain upon all His people in every land of every tongue. The Lord meet in mercy all that seek him. The Lord comfort all that suffer and mourn. The Lord hasten His coming, and now give us and all His people peace by all means.

A Chain of Prayer Across the Ages

110   May the right hand of the Lord keep us ever in old age, the grace of Christ continually defend us from the enemy. O Lord, direct our heart in the way of peace; through Jesus Christ our Lord.

Book of Cerne, 8th Century

111   Now the time has come to part;
Father, come to every heart
Go Thou with us as we go
And be near in all we do.

112   May the Lord Jesus Christ fill us with spiritual joy, may His Spirit make us strong and tranquil in the truths of His promises. And may the blessing of the Lord come upon us abundantly.

A Chain of Prayer Across the Ages

113   The grace of our Lord Jesus Christ, and the love of God, and the fellowship of the Holy Ghost be with us all, evermore.

Eastern Church Liturgy, 1559 A.D.

114   May God, the Lord, bless us with all heavenly benediction, and make us pure and holy in his sight. May the riches of his glory abound in us. May he instruct us with the word of truth, inform us with the Gospel of salvation, and enrich us with his love; through Jesus Christ our Lord.

Gelasian Sacramentary, 6th Century

115   May the blessed Lord be with us, the love of the Eternal Father embrace and follow us. The mighty Savior be our shepherd and defence. The Holy Ghost sanctify, counsel and confirm us, for the praise of Him who called us into His marvellous Light, and into the footsteps of Him who is the Way, the Truth, and the Life, even Jesus Christ our Lord.

A Chain of Prayer Across the Ages

116   Into the faithful hands of our God we commit ourselves now and always. O Lord, let us be thine and remain thine for ever; through Jesus Christ, our Lord.

Book of Prayers for Schools

117   To the Holy Spirit that sanctifies us, with the Father that made and created us, and the Son that redeemed us, be given all honor and glory, world without end.

Thomas Cranmer, 1489–1556

118   May the Lord lead us when we go, and keep us when we sleep, and talk with us when we wake; and may the peace of God, which passeth all understanding, keep our hearts and minds; through Jesus Christ our Lord.

Book of Prayers for Schools

119   The Lord bless all who worship Thee from the rising
of the sun to the going down of the same.
Of thy goodness, give us
With thy love, inspire us
By thy spirit, guide us
By thy power, protect us
In thy mercy receive us, now and always.

Devotional Services

120   And now may the blessing of the Lord rest and remain upon all his people, in every land, of every tongue.

Book of Prayers for Schools

121   Unto the mercies of the holy and glorious Trinity, brethren, we commit you: go ye with the food of your pilgrimage in peace and gladness.

Indian Liturgy

122   May the Lord grant us his blessing and fill our hearts
with the spirit of truth and peace, now and for evermore.

Book of Prayers for Schools

123   Be with us, God the Father,
      Be with us, God the Son,
      Be with us, God the Spirit,
      Eternal Three in One!
      Make us a royal priesthood,
      Thee rightly to adore,
      And fill us with Thy fulness,
      Now and forevermore.

John S. B. Monsell, 1811–1875

124   To thy eternal goodness and mercy do we commend
ourselves, and all who are dear to us. Guard us from evil,
and grant us refreshment and life. Upon every soul in
trouble or darkness do thou cause thy light to shine, that
they may rest in thee, and live in peace.

Book of Prayers for Schools

125   Now may the blessing of God be upon you. May his
truth direct you, and love sustain you; and may He
preserve your going out and your coming in, from this time
forth, and for evermore.

Let Us Worship God

126   May the Lord forgive what we have been; sanctify
what we are; and order what we shall be; for his Name's
sake.

Book of Prayers for Schools

127   Now unto Him who brought His people forth
      Out of the wilderness, by day a cloud
      By night a pillar of fire; to Him alone,
      Look we at last and to no other look we.

Stephen Phillips, 1868–1915

128   May the love of the Lord Jesus draw us to himself;
      May the power of the Lord Jesus strengthen us in his
        service;
      May the joy of the Lord Jesus fill our souls, and
      May the blessing of God Almighty, the Father, the
        Son, and the Holy Spirit, be upon us, and remain
        with us always.

Book of Prayers for Schools

129   Our God and Father, Himself, and our Lord Jesus
Christ, direct our ways; and the Lord make us to increase
and abound in love one towards another, and towards all
men, now and ever.

Book of Prayers for Schools

130   May the Lord give us his servants, in all time of our
life on earth, a mind forgetful of past ill-will, a pure conscience and sincere thoughts, and a heart to love our brothers, for his Name's sake.

Book of Prayers for Schools

131   Go forth into the world in peace; be of good courage;
fight the good fight of faith; that you may finish your course
with joy. And the blessing of God Almighty the Father, the
Son, and the Holy Ghost, be upon us and remain with us
for ever.

The Book of Common Prayer, South Africa

132   Now may God our Father kindle our coldness with the
fire of his love, enlighten our blindness with the brightness
of his presence, and deal mercifully with us, as oftentimes
he has dealt wonderfully with his saints, for Jesus Christ's
sake.

Book of Prayers for Schools

133   To the Lord our God, who hath made the heaven and
the earth by his great power and by his outstretched arm; to
the King of kings and Lord of lords, who only hath the gift
of immortality, dwelling in the light which no man can
approach unto; to the high and holy One that inhabiteth

eternity; be ascribed all might, majesty, dominion and power, henceforth and for evermore.

A. S. T. Fisher

134   May the Father of all mercies, and God of all comfort, support us in all tribulations; that we may be able to strengthen those who are in trouble by the grace wherewith we ourselves are comforted of God.

135   The Lord enrich us with his grace, and further us with his heavenly blessing; the Lord defend us in adversity and keep us from all evil; the Lord receive our prayers, and graciously absolve us from our offences.

Gregorian Sacramentary, 8th Century

136   Into thy hands we commend ourselves. May we be blessed by thy love, and strengthened by thy spirit in all time of our need.

Book of Prayers for Schools

137   Now God himself and our Father and our Lord Jesus Christ make us to increase and abound in love one toward another, and toward all men; that he may establish our hearts unblameable in holiness before him.

138   May God bless us with a loving sense of his near presence, to guide us, to protect us, to help us; that we may know what it is to walk close with him all our life long.

139   Save us, O Lord, waking and guard us sleeping, that awake we may watch with Christ and asleep we may rest in peace.

Book of Prayers for Schools

140   May God the Almighty direct our days in his peace, and grant us the gifts of his blessing; may he deliver us in all our troubles, and establish our minds in tranquillity of his peace, and may he so guide us through the things temporal that we finally lose not the things eternal.

Gregorian Sacramentary, 8th Century

141   May the Almighty God give us grace
        Not only to admire but to obey his doctrine;
        Not only to profess but to practise our faith in him;
    Not only to love but to live his gospel:
        That what we learn of him we may receive into our
            hearts,
        And show forth in our lives,
        Through the might of Jesus Christ our Lord.

142   As we go to our homes, O God, help us to remember what we have learned here, this day, in our church.

143   May the grace of the Lord Jesus Christ sanctify us and keep us from all evil; may he drive far from us all hurtful things, and purify both our souls and bodies; may he bind us to himself by the bond of love, and may his peace abound in our hearts now and for evermore.

                      Gregorian Sacramentary, 8th Century

144   May the grace of courage, gaiety, and the quiet mind, with all such blessedness as belongeth to the children of our heavenly Father, be ours this day; to the praise and glory of his holy Name for evermore.

                      Book of Prayers for Schools

145   Eternal light, shine in our hearts;
        Eternal goodness, deliver us from evil;
        Eternal power, be our support;
        Eternal wisdom, scatter the darkness of our ignorance;
        Eternal pity, have mercy upon us.

                      Alcuin, 735–804

146   The Lord bless us and keep us. The Spirit of the Lord cleanse and purify our inmost hearts, and enable us to shun an evil. The Lord enlighten our understandings and cause the Light of his Truth to shine into our hearts. The Lord fill us with faith and love towards him. The Lord be with us day and night, in our coming in and going out, in our sorrow and in our joy, and bring us at length into his eternal rest.

147   May thy peace, O God . . .
        Wider than our fellowship,
        Deeper than our faith,

Higher than our stars,
Abide in our hearts this day and forever more.

Oscar J. Rumpf

148   Now may the Light that shone in Jesus Christ our Lord,
Shine in our hearts and minds by the indwelling Word;
And may the Radiance which faith and hope restore
Be and abide with us both now and evermore;
And may the Holy Spirit, now to all impart
The incandescence of a love-illumined heart.

Dwight Bradley

149   I beseech you therefore (brothers) by the mercies of God, by the which ye have been made merciful, do that for which you are here present . . . Receive humbly the grace offered to you and use it worthily in all things even to the praise and glory and honour of Him who died for you, Jesus Christ our Lord, who with the Father and the Holy Spirit lives and reigns, Conqueror and Ruler, God glorious for ever, world without end.

Giovanni Parenti, 1227

150   Farewell, spiritual friend(s), you have God's blessing and mine. I pray Almighty God that true peace, perfect guidance, spiritual strength and an abundance of grace may evermore be with you and all God's lovers on earth.

The Cloud of Unknowing

151   May God's love and care
Be with you
And be seen in you
This week, and always. Amen.

152   The God of all love, who is the source of our affection for each other, take our friendships into his own keeping; that they may continue and increase throughout life and beyond it.

William Temple, 1881–1944

153   And now, brethren, farewell. Be perfect, be of good comfort, be of one mind, live in peace; and the God of love and peace be with you.

Let Us Worship God

154   And unto thee, O Father, we commit not only ourselves but all those who are dear to us, wherever they may
be. Grant to them rest, and protection from all dangers of
the night. Forgive them and us for any failures of the day,
and especially for any sins against love. Help us more and
more to learn our need of one another, and above all our
need of thee, O Love that will not let us go.

Walter R. Bowie, 1882–

155   O Christ, Revealer of the Father,
   Reveal thyself in us.
   O Christ, who didst illumine the darkness of men's
      despair,
   Make us believe in light.
   O Christ, who dared to seem reflected on the Cross,
   Make us believe in love.
   O Christ, invincible in sacrifice, risen and immortal,
   Make us believe in God triumphant in all life.
   And unto God the Father, God the Son, and God the
      Holy Spirit, be ascribed all might, majesty, domin-
      ion, and power, both now and evermore.

Walter R. Bowie, 1882–

156   And now may the blessings of the Lord rest upon all
His people in every land, of every tongue. The Lord meet in
mercy all that seek Him. The Lord comfort all that suffer
and mourn. The Lord hasten His coming and give us and all
His people peace both now and forever more.

157   May the glad dawn of Easter morn
   Bring joy to thee.
   May the calm eve of Easter leave
   A peace divine with thee,
   May Easter night on thine heart write,
   O Christ, I live for thee.

158   May it be Thy will, our God and God of our fathers,
that this coming year be unto all thy people a year of plenty,
a year of blessings, a year of assembly in thy sanctuary, a
year of happy life from Thee, a year of dew and rain and
warmth, a year in which Thou wilt bless our bread and
water, a year in which thy mercies will be moved toward us,

a year of peace and tranquility in which Thou wilt set a blessing upon the work of our hands.

Ancient Hebrew Prayer

159   May the Almighty God, who by the Incarnation of His only begotten Son, has chased away the darkness of the world, and irradiated this sacred night with His glorious Nativity, chase far from you the darkness of sin, and irradiate your hearts with the light of virtue. Amen.

160   And may He, the great Shepherd, who willed that the joy of His blessed Nativity should be made known to shepherds by an Angel, pour upon you the refreshing dew of His benediction, and Himself lead you to the pastures of eternal joy. Amen.

161   And may He, who by His Incarnation united things earthly and heavenly, fill you with the sweetness of inward peace and good will, and make you comrades of the heavenly Host. Amen.

Gregorian Sacramentary, 8th Century

Index of Topics
and Special Occasions

235